ADVENTURING
through the
LIFE *of*
CHRIST

A Bible Handbook on the Gospels and Acts

ADVENTURING
through the
LIFE *of*
CHRIST

RAY C. STEDMAN

DISCOVERY HOUSE
PUBLISHERS®

Discovery House Publishers is affiliated with RBC Ministries, Grand Rapids, Michigan.

Discovery House books are distributed to the trade exclusively by Barbour Publishing, Inc., Uhrichsville, Ohio.

Requests for permission to quote from this book should be directed to: Permissions Department, Discovery House Publishers, P.O. Box 3566, Grand Rapids, MI 49501.

Unless otherwise indicated, Scripture quotations are from the HOLY BIBLE: NEW INTERNATIONAL VERSION®. NIV® Copyright © 1973, 1978, 1984 by Biblica, Inc.™ Used by permission of Zondervan. All rights reserved worldwide. www.zondervan.com

Interior design by Veldheer Creative Services

ISBN: 978-1-57293-311-8

Printed in the United States of America

10 11 12 / BPI / 10 9 8 7 6 5 4 3

CONTENTS

ADVENTURING
through the
LIFE *of* CHRIST

CHAPTER ONE

MATTHEW
through ACTS:
JESUS *and*
HIS CHURCH

T HROUGHOUT THE PAGES of the Old Testament, we read about Jesus Christ. Even though He is never named in the Old Testament, He appears on almost every page in the form of symbols, shadows, types, rituals, sacrifices, and prophecies. As we turn to the pages of the New Testament, however, we encounter Him in the flesh. Here, in the form of a living, breathing human being, is the one who satisfies and fulfills all the symbols and prophecies of Genesis through Malachi. As we move from the Old Testament to the New, we find that one person, Jesus of Nazareth, is the focal point of both Testaments.

> **We encounter this man, Jesus Christ, through four separate portraits—Matthew, Mark, Luke, and John.**

We encounter this man, Jesus Christ, through four separate portraits—Matthew, Mark, Luke, and John. Many have asked, "Why is it necessary to have four Gospels instead of just one? Why couldn't one of these writers have gotten all the facts together and presented them for us in one book?" Well, that would be like trying to use one photograph of a building to adequately represent the entire structure. One picture could not possibly show all four sides of the building at once.

The same is true of Jesus. His life, His character, and His ministry are so rich and multifaceted that a single view could not tell the whole story. God deliberately planned for four Gospels so that each could present our Lord in a unique way. Each Gospel presents a distinct aspect of Christ, and our understanding of who He truly is would be incalculably poorer if even one of these Gospels was lost to us.

The Fourfold Image of Christ

Matthew: Jesus the King

The Old Testament is filled with pictures of the coming Messiah, and these pictures correspond with the portraits of Jesus "painted" for us in the four Gospels. First, He is pictured in many prophecies—particularly those of Isaiah, Jeremiah, and Zechariah—as the coming King of Israel. For obvious reasons, the people of Israel have loved that picture—which is one of the principle reasons why Israel rejected the Lord when He came: He did not look like the king of their expectations. But Matthew, in his Gospel, saw the kingly aspects of Jesus and His ministry, and those are the aspects he emphasized. Matthew, then, is the Gospel of the King.

Mark: Jesus the Suffering Servant

Second, Jesus the Messiah was portrayed in many parts of the Old Testament as the servant, the suffering one. We see these images of the suffering servant especially in Isaiah. Joseph, in the book of Genesis, is also seen as a type of the One who would come to suffer and serve. The Hebrews found these two images of the Messiah so confusing—the Messiah-King versus the suffering Messiah-Servant—that many Jewish scholars concluded that there must be two Messiahs. They called one "Messiah Ben-David," or Messiah the son of David, and the other "Messiah Ben-Joseph," or Messiah the son of Joseph. Messiah Ben-David was viewed as the kingly Messiah, while Messiah Ben-Joseph was the suffering one. They couldn't imagine that the king and the servant could be the same person! But Mark understood the humble, self-sacrificing, servant nature of Christ, and that is the aspect he presents to us in his Gospel.

Third, we have frequent Old Testament pictures of Christ's coming as a man. He was to be born of a virgin, grow up in Bethlehem, and walk among human beings. He was to be the perfect human being. That is also the image presented to us by Luke in his Gospel. *Luke: Jesus the Perfect Human Being*

Finally, we have those Old Testament pictures that speak of the Messiah as God, as the Everlasting One. For example, Micah 5:2 predicts that the Messiah will come out of the small town of Bethlehem Ephrathah—where Jesus was, in fact, born—and that Messiah's origins are from everlasting (that is, He has no beginning, He is eternal, He is God). This accords with the picture of Jesus that we derive from the Gospel of John, the Gospel of the Son of God. *John: Jesus the Everlasting One*

So all of the Old Testament prophecies and pictures of Christ can be placed under these four Gospel headings: king, servant, human being, and God. Interestingly enough, in four places in the Old Testament (in the King James Version) the word *behold* is used in connection with one of these four pictures. In Zechariah 9:9, God says to the daughters of Zion and Jerusalem, "Behold, thy King cometh" (KJV). That prophecy was fulfilled when our Lord entered Jerusalem in triumph. Then in Isaiah 42:1, God says, "Behold my servant" (KJV). It is not "thy servant" but "my servant." Christ is not the servant of humanity but the servant of God. In Zechariah 6:12, the Lord says, "Behold, the man" (KJV). He is speaking in this passage about the Messiah. And in Isaiah 40:9, He says, "Say unto the cities of Judah, Behold your God!" (KJV). Four times that phrase is used, each time in connection with a different aspect of Christ. So we can clearly see that God has woven a marvelous and consistent pattern into His Word, both the Old Testament and the New. This pattern reveals the many facets and dimensions of Jesus the Messiah.

> **Christ is not the servant of humanity but the servant of God.**

Unity, Not Harmony

It is fascinating to notice all the techniques, details, and nuances used by each Gospel writer to paint his unique and individual portrait of Jesus Christ.

Matthew, the Gospel of the King

In Matthew, the Gospel of the King, we see many evidences of His kingship: The book opens with Christ's genealogy, tracing His royal line back to David, king of Israel, and to Abraham, father of the nation Israel. Throughout the book, He speaks and acts with kingly authority: "Moses said to you so-and-so, but I say to you such-and-such." To the Jews, Moses was the great authority, so for Jesus to supersede the authority of Moses was to act as a king. He demonstrated the authority to dismiss evil spirits and command the sick to be healed and the blind to see. With kingly authority, He passed judgment on the officials of the nation, saying, "Woe to you, scribes and Pharisees, hypocrites!" The key phrase Jesus uses again and again through Matthew's Gospel is "the kingdom of heaven"—it occurs thirty-two times in Matthew. Matthew is constantly referring to the kingdom of heaven and the King. In his account of our Lord's birth, Matthew says that Christ was born King of the Jews, and in his account of the crucifixion, he says that Jesus was crucified as King of the Jews.

Mark, the Gospel of the Servant

Mark, the second Gospel, pictures Christ as the Servant, and as you would expect, Mark does not provide any genealogy for Christ. After all, who cares about the genealogy of a servant? Nobody. In Mark's Gospel, our Lord simply appears on the scene. Again and again in this Gospel, we see the word *immediately*. That is the word of a servant, isn't it? When you give a servant an order, you want it carried out immediately, not ten minutes later. So again and again we read, "Immediately, Jesus did so-and-so." Whereas both Luke and Matthew are filled with parables on many subjects and issues, Mark, the Gospel of the Servant, contains only four parables—and each of them is a parable of servanthood. They represent Jesus as the Servant of Jehovah—the suffering servant pictured in Isaiah 53. Read through the Gospel of Mark and you will never see Jesus called *Lord* until after His resurrection—another mark of His servant role. Mark 13:32 is a verse that profoundly illustrates His servanthood—and a verse that has puzzled many. In that verse, our Lord says of His second coming:

> *"No one knows about that day or hour, not even the angels in heaven, nor the Son, but only the Father."*

How could Jesus be the omnipotent God and still not know the time of

His own return? This is a total mystery until you understand the character of Mark's Gospel. Mark describes Christ in His role as the suffering servant of God. It is not a servant's place to know what his Lord is doing—even when that servant is the Son of God Himself.

Luke shows us Christ as human. Here we see the perfection of His manhood—the glory, beauty, strength, and dignity of His humanity. As *Luke, the Gospel of the Son of Man* we would expect, Luke also contains a genealogy of Christ. If Jesus is to be presented as human, we want to know that He belongs to the human race. And Luke makes this case for Christ's complete identification with Adam's race by tracing His genealogy all the way back to Adam. In Luke, we find Christ often in prayer. If you want to see Jesus at prayer, read the Gospel of Luke. Prayer is a picture of humanity's proper relationship to God—total dependence upon the sovereign, omnipotent God. In Luke, we see His human sympathy most clearly—His weeping over the city of Jerusalem, His healing of the man whose ear Peter cut off when the soldiers arrested Jesus in the garden. No other Gospel relates these two incidents that so powerfully show the sympathetic, human aspect of our Lord. Luke also relates the fullest account of Christ's agony in the garden where He sweats drops of blood, so eloquently symbolic of the human being who fully enters into our trials and pain.

> **If you want to see Jesus at prayer, read the Gospel of Luke.**

John's Gospel presents Christ as God. From the very first verse, this is John's potent, unmistakable theme. Many people fail to realize that John's *John, the Gospel of the Son of God* Gospel, like Matthew's and Luke's, opens with a genealogy. The reason so many people miss the genealogy in John is that it is so short:

> *In the beginning was the Word, and the Word was with God, and the Word was God (1:1).*

That's it! That's John's entire genealogy of Christ—two people, the Father and the Son. Why is this genealogy so short? Because John's purpose is so simple: to set forth the account of Christ's divine nature. In John's Gospel we see seven "I am" declarations (I have listed them in chapter 6). These seven declarations echo the great statement of the Lord to Moses from the burning bush, "I AM WHO I AM" (Ex. 3:14).

In addition to these seven dramatic "I am" declarations, we read about an incident in the garden where the "I am" statement of Jesus has a powerful impact. It happens when Judas leads the soldiers to the garden to arrest Jesus. When the soldiers tell the Lord that they are seeking a man called

Jesus of Nazareth, He responds, "I am he," and the force of that great "I am" declaration—a declaration of His own godhood—is so powerful that the soldiers fall back in stunned amazement (see John 18:3–8)!

In John 20:30–31, the writer clearly states that his purpose is not to set down an exhaustive biography of the Lord but to inspire saving belief in the godhood of Jesus Christ, the Son of God:

> *Jesus did many other miraculous signs in the presence of his disciples, which are not recorded in this book. But these are written that you may believe that Jesus is the Christ, the Son of God, and that by believing you may have life in his name.*

Finally, before we move on to examine these four Gospels individually, we should note that it is impossible to chronologically harmonize these accounts because they are not intended to be chronological accounts. Matthew, Mark, Luke, and John did not sit down to record a chronological biography of Jesus. They wrote to present specific aspects of the Lord's life and ministry, but none of these books claims to be a chronology of His life. Though we cannot precisely harmonize these events, however, it is possible to obtain a fairly reliable general sequence of events by comparing the Gospels, especially if we rely on John's Gospel, which appears to be the most chronologically precise of the four.

The Book of Acts

You might think I've just thrown Acts into this handbook with the Gospels because it doesn't fit with the epistles. No, I have deliberately included Acts with the Gospels because it continues their story. Written by Luke, it is really a sequel to Luke's Gospel, but it actually serves as a fitting sequel to all four Gospels. While the Gospels tell the story of Christ in His earthly body, in His ministry on earth, the book of Acts tells the story of the body of Christ, the church, which continues His work on earth after His ascension into heaven.

Acts, a Fitting Sequel to the Gospels and the Key to the New Testament

In many ways, Acts is the key to the New Testament. We couldn't understand the New Testament if this book were left out. The four Gospels teach us that the apostles have been sent to preach the gospel to Israel—and only Israel. But in Acts we learn of God's command that the gospel be taken into all the world, to the Gentiles as well as the house of Israel. If we leave out the book of Acts and skip directly to the epistles, we find that another apostle has mysteriously been added—some fellow named Paul! Instead of talking about God's kingdom, Christians are talking about a new organization—the church. Instead of a gospel that is confined to Jews in the region around the city of Jerusalem, Christianity has spread—in the short span of a single generation—to the limits of the then-known world! We would be puzzled as to where this church and this apostle Paul came from, and we would wonder how this incredible spread of Christianity has taken place. All of this is explained in the book of Acts.

> The key to understanding Acts is the realization that this book is not a record of the acts of the apostles but the acts of the Lord Jesus Christ!

The key to understanding Acts is the realization that this book is not a record of the acts of the apostles but the acts of the Lord Jesus Christ! Notice how the book begins:

In my former book, Theophilus, I wrote about all that Jesus began to do and to teach (1:1).

Notice Luke's choice of words! In the Gospel of Luke, he recorded what the Lord Jesus began to do. But now, in Acts, Luke gives us the record of what our Lord is continuing to do. So it is the Lord who is at work throughout both books. Luke is volume one; Acts is volume two.

During World War II, Britain's prime minister, Winston Churchill, broadcast an announcement of the victories of the allied forces when they had swept across North Africa and were about to launch the invasion of Sicily. Churchill summed up his announcement with these words: "This is not the end. This is not even the beginning of the end. But it may be the end of the beginning." That is what we have in the four Gospels. It is not the end of our Lord's ministry when He ascends into the heavens, as Luke records in Acts 1. That is just the end of the beginning. But in the rest of Acts we have the beginning of the end.

Throughout the book of Acts, we have the record of Christ's continuing ministry through the instrumentality of men and women who are just like you and me. In Luke 12:50, shortly before the cross, Jesus tells His disciples, "I have a baptism to undergo, and how distressed I am until it is completed!" That is, "How limited and shackled I am until this thing is accomplished!" Well, it has been accomplished now. Our Lord is no longer limited and shackled. When He ascended into heaven, the Holy Spirit came to us, His followers. The omnipotence of God was unleashed in the lives of ordinary men and women, enabling them to do extraordinary things in His name.

That is why we have the tremendous explosion of ministry power: the book of Acts.

Acts is the one book of the Bible that is not yet finished. Notice that it ends abruptly. The last two verses say that Paul has reached Rome:

> *For two whole years Paul stayed there in his own rented house and welcomed all who came to see him. Boldly and without hindrance he preached the kingdom of God and taught about the Lord Jesus Christ (28:30–31).*

I never close this book without wondering to myself, "Well, what happened next?" The book of Acts leaves you hanging. It gives the distinct impression of being unfinished. And there is a reason for this. It is because this is the biography of a living person—Jesus Christ. The last chapter of His story has not yet been written.

I have in my library an autobiography of Dr. H. A. Ironside, and it ends on the same sort of note. It leaves you hanging. You wonder what happens next. It isn't complete because, at the time it was written, his life hadn't ended.

The book of Acts continues to be written today in the lives of men and women in the living body of Christ, the church. Even though Jesus has been taken up in the clouds, His body life goes on! It goes on in your life. It goes on in my life. It goes on and on, outliving and outlasting the lives and institutions of mere mortals, of nations, of civilizations. Rome has fallen, the empires of the Huns, the Mongols, the Aztecs, the Manchu Chinese, and the British have all risen and declined. Colonialism has collapsed in the Americas, Africa, and Asia; Soviet communism has come and gone; two world wars have been fought; we have gone from the Dark Ages to the Internet Age—and still the body life of Jesus Christ goes on, the book of Acts continues to be written. You and I are still writing the book of Acts today because it is an account of what the Holy Spirit continues to do through us today, all around the world.

> The book of Acts continues to be written today in the lives of men and women in the living body of Christ, the church.

We are the body of Christ. We are His miracle-working, ministering hands of service; we are His eyes of compassion and love; we are His voice of truth, calling the world to repentance and faith in Him; we are His feet, swift to carry His message around the world. His body life goes on and on and on. We are still writing the book of the Acts of Jesus Christ in the New Testament age. We haven't seen the last page yet.

So as we study the five books of His life—Matthew, Mark, Luke, John, and Acts—let us view them as a guide to our own way of life as we seek to let Him live His life through us.

NOTES

NOTES

_____

_____

_____

_____

_____

_____

_____

_____

_____

_____

_____

_____

_____

_____

_____

_____

_____

_____

_____

NOTES

NOTES

NOTES

NOTES

ADVENTURING
through the
LIFE *of* CHRIST

CHAPTER TWO

MATTHEW:
BEHOLD
YOUR KING!

NEARLY A CENTURY AGO, an Englishman named Greene was walking through the woods when he came upon a stranger in the path. He was startled when the stranger smiled and waved at him. "Oh, hello, Mr. Greene!" said the stranger. Obviously this "stranger" wasn't a stranger at all—but for the life of him, Mr. Greene could not place him.

Embarrassed, but unwilling to admit to a poor memory for names and faces, Mr. Greene offered his hand. "Ah, yes! Hello! Good to see you, old boy! How long has it been?"

"Well," said the other man, "it was at Lady Asquith's reception last October, wasn't it? Nearly a year, then."

Mr. Greene remembered Lady Asquith's reception and tried to recall all the people he had met. This gentleman's face looked familiar, but he just couldn't place it. Still groping for clues to this fellow's identity, Greene decided to ask a few questions. "And how is your wife?"

"Quite well," said the other man.

"And you? Still in the same business, I presume?"

"Oh, yes," said the other man, with a merry twinkle in his eye. "I'm still the king of England."

Mr. Greene, behold your king!

That is the message of the Gospel of Matthew to you and me: Behold your king! Until we have closely examined Jesus' credentials as the King of creation and Lord of our lives, as presented in this Gospel, we will not fully recognize Him in all His glory.

Astonished by the Gospels

The Old Testament is shadow. The New Testament is sunshine.

The Old Testament is type and symbol. The New Testament is reality and substance.

The Old Testament is prophecy. The New Testament is fulfillment.

In the Old Testament, we must piece together a complex mosaic of Christ. In the New Testament, Jesus blazes from the page in three-dimensional realism.

> The Old Testament is type and symbol. The New Testament is reality and substance.

Though the Old Testament speaks of Him on almost every page, it speaks in shadows, types, symbols, and prophecies that anticipate the coming of Someone. You cannot read the Old Testament without being aware of that constant promise running through every page: Someone is coming! Someone is coming!

But as we open the Gospels, it becomes clear that the long-awaited moment has come. That promised and prophesied Someone has arrived—and He steps forth in all the astonishing fullness of His glory. As John says, "We have seen his glory, the glory of the One and Only, who came from the Father, full of grace and truth" (John 1:14).

I love the Gospels. They are the most fascinating section of the Bible to me because they are the eyewitness accounts of the life of that wonderful Someone around whom all the rest of the Bible revolves. In the Gospels, we see Christ as He is. The Gospels confront us with the fact that what He is may not always be what we think He is or what we would like Him to be. He is startling, He is awesome. No matter how many times we read the Gospels, He continues to astonish us and challenge our assumptions about Him.

If you are a Christian, a follower of Christ, then all that He is, you have. All the fullness of His character and life is available to you. We learn what those resources are as we see Him as He was—and as He is. That is why the Gospel accounts are so important to us.

The Synoptic Gospels

Matthew, along with Mark and Luke, is one of the Synoptic Gospels (*synoptic* means "viewed together"). Although all four Gospels complement and reinforce each other, the style, theme, and viewpoint of the three Synoptic Gospels differ from that of John. Read in parallel, the three synoptics impress us with many similarities and overlapping detail, although each Gospel has its own distinct atmosphere, voice, and style. The fourth Gospel, John, while noticeably different in approach and purpose, tone and detail from the first three, provides a complementary view of the life of Christ.

The Gospel of Matthew is written to present Christ as the King. The Gospel of Mark presents His character as a Servant. The Gospel of Luke presents Him as the Son of Man. The Gospel of John presents Him as the Son of God, and there you find the greatest claims for His deity.

Jesus from Four Perspectives

Each of these Gospels was addressed to a specific audience. Matthew wrote his Gospel primarily for the Jews, and it is filled with references and quotations from the Old Testament. Luke wrote his Gospel for the Greek mind, the philosophical mind, and it is filled with the Lord's table talk, as He sat with His disciples in intimate fellowship, exploring realms of spiritual truth—the Greeks loved this. Mark wrote his Gospel for the Roman mind; it contains

> Each of these Gospels was addressed to a specific audience.

the most Latin words. It is also the Gospel of haste and action, which are characteristics of the Roman spirit. And John wrote his Gospel for the Christian, which is why the Gospel of John is dearest to Christian hearts; it not only emphasizes the deity of Christ, but unveils the teaching of the rapture of the church, the intimacy of fellowship and communion between the Lord and His own, and the ministry of the Holy Spirit.

> If you understand that the four Gospels were written for four different purposes, from four different perspectives, to four different audiences, you will understand why you find certain differences among them.

If you understand that the four Gospels were written for four different purposes, from four different perspectives, to four different audiences, you will understand why you find certain differences among them. For example, people often wonder why John's Gospel doesn't mention the struggle of our Lord in Gethsemane. We find the record of Gethsemane's agony in Matthew, Mark, and Luke, but nothing about it in John. The answer, in light of the Holy Spirit's purpose for each unique Gospel, is clear: It is because in the Garden of Gethsemane, Jesus cried out and questioned the Father, "If it be possible, let this cup pass from me." Now, it is not Jesus in His role as the Son of God who questions the Father, because God cannot question God. It is Jesus in His humanity who does this, so the Gethsemane account is found in Matthew, Mark, and Luke, which present the most complete and compelling record of His human struggle. In John, the Gospel of the Son of God, this record is omitted. This is not a discrepancy or a contradiction among the Gospels; it is simply a difference in theme and emphasis.

Another example: Matthew directs our attention to the wise men who came to offer their gifts to the baby Jesus, while Luke focuses on the pilgrimage of the shepherds. Now, both wise men and shepherds came to honor the baby Jesus, but in Matthew—the Gospel of the King—the wise men brought gifts fit for a king. In Luke—the Gospel of the Son of Man—common, ordinary shepherds came to see the perfect human, the one who came to be among us, equal with us, on our level.

Why is there no account of the ascension of our Lord in Matthew and John, as there is in Mark and Luke? Because as King, Jesus came to rule on earth, and Matthew's emphasis is on the kingdom on earth. The ascension is not mentioned in John, because Jesus is the Son of God, and God is always everywhere.

Why do Mark and John omit a lengthy genealogy of our Lord? You'll find a lengthy genealogy in Matthew, the Gospel of the King, because kings require royal genealogies. A lengthy genealogy also opens Luke, the Gospel of the Son of Man, because human beings are interested in their ancestry, in their origins. But you'll see no lengthy genealogy in John, the Gospel of the Son of God, because God has no ancestry; He is eternal. No genealogy is recorded in Mark, the Gospel of the Servant, because no one cares about the ancestry of a servant.

All of this shows the supervision of the Holy Spirit. These Gospels are not merely copies of one another. The Holy Spirit deliberately designed the uniqueness of each Gospel as well as the unity of the four Gospels. We make a mistake if we think these four Gospels are four biographies of the Lord, intended to be the complete life and times of Jesus Christ. They are not biographies but character sketches, intended to present different points of view, different dimensions of the complex and endlessly fascinating person of the Lord Jesus Christ.

As you read the Gospel accounts, I hope you experience something of the tremendous impact of the most powerful human personality in history. There is no more transforming, life-changing experience in all of life than the experience of seeing Jesus as He truly is, as He is revealed on the pages of the Gospels and by the Holy Spirit.

Stamped with the Fingerprints of God

The first book of the New Testament is Matthew. Most people, I believe, begin reading in the New Testament rather than the Old, and most begin at the beginning of the New Testament. Matthew, then, is probably the most widely read book of the Bible. Renan, the French skeptic, called this book "the most important book of all Christendom."

The Gospel of Matthew has its critics, too. There are those who claim that this book contains nothing but the early legends of the church that grew up around Jesus but are not historical and that this book was not actually written until the fourth century A.D. Therefore, they say, we are uncertain as to how much is really true. Other critics claim that Matthew is only one of many gospels that were propagated in the early Christian era.

It is true that other "gospels" were circulated, besides the four in the New Testament. Gospels supposedly were written by Barnabas or Peter or Thomas and even Pontius Pilate! In fact, you can find more than a hundred documents called "the New Testament Apocrypha," consisting of fanciful gospels, epistles, and prophecies (the word *apocryphal* originally meant "hidden," but it has also come to mean "of doubtful authenticity"). You can find these New Testament Apocrypha at your local public library if you would like to read them, and in most cases, you can sense simply by reading them that they are absurd and far-fetched and do not belong in the accepted canon of Scripture. Many of them were generated by adherents of the gnostic heresy that was rampant during the early Christian era.

Some critics say it is mere chance that our four Gospels survived and were chosen as part of our New Testament. One legend began with a German theologian named Pappas in about the sixteenth century, who claimed that the Gospels were selected at the Council of Nicaea in A.D. 325 by gathering together all the gospels in circulation at that time, throwing them under a table, then reaching in and pulling out these four: Matthew, Mark, Luke, and John. The foolishness of such a claim is evident to anyone who reads the Gospels with thoughtfulness and care. These four books bear the fingerprints of God. The very pattern of these books reflects the divine imprint, and you cannot read them or compare them with the Old Testament without seeing that they come from an inspired source.

> **These four books [the Gospels] bear the fingerprints of God.**

The Author and Date of Matthew

The first of the four New Testament Gospels was written by Matthew, also known as Levi. He was a tax collector before he became a follower of Christ. Since his name, Matthew, means "the gift of God," it is probably a new name given him after his conversion. Perhaps it is even a name given him by our Lord Himself, just as Jesus changed Simon's name to Peter. Scholars believe that Matthew lived and taught in Palestine for fifteen years after the crucifixion, and then he began to travel as a missionary, first to Ethiopia and then to Macedonia, Syria, and Persia. Scholars also believe that he died a natural death in either Ethiopia or Macedonia, but this is not certain.

The book was written in the first century A.D., possibly in the early half of the first century. It is quoted, for instance, in the well-known *Didache*, the teaching of the twelve apostles that dates from early in the second century. Papias, a disciple of the apostle John, says, "Matthew composed his Gospel in the Hebrew tongue, and each one interprets it as he is able." This was confirmed by Irenaeus and Origen, two early church fathers who were well acquainted with the Gospel of Matthew.

Even in the first century we have Jewish voices that prove the early existence of Matthew. Two Jewish people, Gamaliel the Second, a prominent rabbi, and his sister, Immashalom (which, incidentally, means "woman of peace," though she wasn't) pronounced a curse upon Christians as "readers of the evangelistic scriptures." Since the only evangelistic Scriptures extant in their day (about A.D. 45 or 50) were the Gospel of Matthew and, perhaps, the Gospel of Mark, the date of the writing of this Gospel would have to be about A.D. 45 or 50. It likely was first written in Hebrew, then translated into Greek.

The Structure of Matthew

The Holy Spirit Himself has given the outline of the Gospel of Matthew, as He does in several other books of Scripture. The major divisions of Matthew are marked by the repetition of a particular phrase that appears twice and divides the book into three sections. First, there is an introductory section, the coming of the king, chapters 1 to 4. Then, at the beginning of the second section, in 4:17, we find the phrase "from that time on":

> From that time on Jesus began to preach, "Repent, for the kingdom of heaven is near."

That statement marks a major turning point in the argument and presentation of this book. We find an identical phrase occurring in 16:21, introducing the third section:

> From that time on Jesus began to explain to his disciples that he must go to Jerusalem and suffer many things at the hands of the elders, chief priests and teachers of the law, and that he must be killed and on the third day be raised to life.

That is the first mention of the crucifixion in Matthew, and from this point forward, the cross is (literally) the crux of this book.

There are also subdivisions in Matthew, which are marked off by the phrase "when [or, "after"] Jesus had finished." The first is found in 7:28–29, at the close of the Sermon on the Mount:

> From this point forward, the cross is (literally) the crux of this book.

When Jesus had finished saying these things, the crowds were amazed at his teaching, because he taught as one who had authority, and not as their teachers of the law.

In 11:1, another subdivision is indicated:

After Jesus had finished instructing his twelve disciples, he went on from there to teach and preach in the towns of Galilee.

In 13:53–54, another subdivision is indicated:

When Jesus had finished these parables, he moved on from there. Coming to his hometown, he began teaching the people in their synagogue, and they were amazed. "Where did this man get this wisdom and these miraculous powers?" they asked.

In 19:1–2, another subdivision:

When Jesus had finished saying these things, he left Galilee and went into the region of Judea to the other side of the Jordan. Large crowds followed him, and he healed them there.

Notice that each of these subsections introduces a complete change of direction in the Lord's ministry and in the direction of the book. These mark the divisions of the Gospel of Matthew.

The Outline of Matthew, the Gospel of the King

The Coming of the King (Matthew 1:1–4:16)

1.	The royal genealogy	1:1–17
2.	The birth of King Jesus	1:18–25
3.	The visit of the wise men	2:1–12
4.	Escape into Egypt and slaughter of the innocents	2:13–23
5.	John the Baptist announces and baptizes the King	3:1–17
6.	The temptation of the King in the wilderness	4:1–16

19.	The cursing of the fig tree	21:18–22
20.	Conflict with the religious leaders	21:23–23:39
21.	Predictions of the second coming of the King	24–25
22.	The Lord's Supper and the betrayal of the King	26:1–35
23.	Jesus arrested in the garden, tried before Caiaphas and Pilate	26:36–27:25
24.	The crucifixion of the King	27:26–66
25.	The empty tomb	28:1–8
26.	Jesus appears to the women and the disciples	28:9–17
27.	The Great Commission	28:18–20

Matthew is the Gospel of the King, and the first division of the book (Matt. 1:1–4:16) is about the preparation of the King for His ministry. Because Matthew's task is to present Jesus as the King, the book opens with the genealogy of the King.

The Genealogy of the King

Every king has to have a genealogy. The ancestry of a king is the most important thing about him. His right of kingship is based on his royal lineage. So Matthew opens with that exhaustive and somewhat exhausting genealogy, tracing the ancestry of Jesus from Abraham on down to Joseph, His stepfather, who was the husband of Mary and was in the royal line of David. Our Lord gets His royal right to the throne from Joseph, because He was the heir of Joseph. Jesus gets His genealogical right to the throne through Mary, who was also of the royal line of David. Jesus' legal right comes through Joseph, His hereditary right through Mary. Joseph, of course, was not His actual father, but Mary really was His mother.

> **Jesus' legal right comes through Joseph, His hereditary right through Mary.**

The first chapter also recounts His birth. The second chapter describes events following His birth, including the escape into Egypt after Herod decreed the slaughter of the innocents in an effort to destroy this rival king, the baby Jesus. In the third chapter we read of the baptism of our Lord.

The first two chapters of Matthew establish the earthly connection of Jesus—His royal lineage and human birth. These chapters anchor Him in human history, in time and space. In the third chapter, His baptism establishes His heavenly connection, His heavenly credentials, and His heavenly authority. In chapter 3, the heavens open and God the Father speaks from heaven, declaring Jesus to be His beloved Son. At that moment, the royal line of Jesus is established not according to a human bloodline but according to the heavenly standard. Jesus is King by right of being the Son of the Creator-King of the universe.

The Testing of Jesus in His Humanity

In Matthew 4, we witness the testing of the King in the wilderness, where He is permitted to be tempted by all the powers of darkness. Hungry, weary, and alone, Jesus is left in a place where hell is loosed upon Him, where Satan himself is permitted to take his best shot. The testing of our Lord is the key to the Gospel of Matthew, for He is tested as a representative human being. He goes into the wilderness as the Son of Man and is tested as to whether or not He can fulfill God's intention for humanity. Humans are made up of body, soul, and spirit, and Jesus is tested in the wilderness on each of these three levels.

He was tested first on the level of the body's demands. The dominant passion of the body is self-preservation, and our Lord's first temptation came on that most basic level. Would He continue to be God's person, even when faced by an extreme challenge to His very life? For forty days and nights He had not eaten, and then the temptation came subtly to Him: "The tempter came to him and said, 'If you are the Son of God, tell these stones to become bread' "(4:3). But He steadfastly remained in the Father's will despite His great hunger and need. — *His Body Was Tested*

Next, Jesus was tested on the level of the soul—that is, through the dominant passion of the soul, which is self-expression. On this level, we all desire to reveal our egos, to show what we can do, to express ourselves. This is the primary drive of the human soul. It was during this testing that our Lord was taken up to the top of the temple and given the opportunity to cast Himself down and thus capture the acclaim of Israel. Such temptation plays upon the urge for status, for manifesting the pride of life. But Jesus proved Himself true to God despite the pressure that came to Him in that way. — *His Soul Was Tested*

Finally, He was tested in the deepest, most essential part of His humanity—the spirit. The dominant passion of the human spirit is to worship. The spirit is always looking for something to worship. That is why human beings are essentially religious beings; the spirit in them is craving, is crying out for an idol, a hero, something or someone to worship and be in awe of. It was on this level that the devil next came to Jesus: — *His Spirit Was Tested*

Again, the devil took him to a very high mountain and showed him all the kingdoms of the world and their splendor. "All this I will give you," he said, "if you will bow down and worship me."

Jesus said to him, "Away from me, Satan! For it is written: 'Worship the Lord your God, and serve him only.' "

Then the devil left him, and angels came and attended him (4:8–11).

So Jesus passed the threefold test. He revealed Himself fully and adequately to be human as God intended humanity to be.

In the Sermon on the Mount (5–7), Jesus begins to put this same test to the nation Israel. Throughout the Old Testament, we see that God had chosen Israel to be His channel of communication with humanity and that the people of Israel regarded themselves as God's favored people. Now the nation is put to the test—the same test, in fact, that Jesus Himself has just passed.

This is the essence of Matthew's Gospel. He is tracing for us the way God's King came into the world, offered Himself as King of Israel—first on the level of the physical, then on the level of the soul. When He was rejected on both these levels, He passed into the realm of the mystery of the human spirit. In the darkness and mystery of the cross, He accomplished the redeeming work that would restore human beings to their Creator—body, soul, and spirit.

Redemption, therefore, begins with the spirit. The work of Christ in our own lives does not really change us until it has reached the level of our spirits, the source of our worship. We may be attracted to Christ on the level of the body, because He supplies our physical need for safety, shelter, and daily sustenance. Or we may be attracted to Him on the level of the soul, because He satisfies our need for affirmation, self-esteem, and self-expression. But if our relationship with Christ does not penetrate our lives to the deep recesses of the spirit, we have not truly been permeated and changed by His life. We must be wholly committed to Him—body, soul, and spirit.

> If our relationship with Christ does not penetrate our lives to the deep recesses of the spirit, we have not truly been permeated and changed by His life.

Israel Is Tested in the Physical Realm

Jesus' ministry begins, as we saw in 4:17, with the words, "From that time on Jesus began to preach, 'Repent, for the kingdom of heaven is near.' " Then follows the Sermon on the Mount, where we have the presentation of the King and the laws of the kingdom. This covers the rest of chapters 4 and 5 through 7. In these rules for life in the kingdom, laid down in the Sermon on the Mount, the obvious emphasis is on the physical life.

This is one of the most penetrating and incisive messages ever set before human beings, and it approaches us on the level of our ordinary, physical lives. Two physical sins are dealt with here: murder and adultery. The life of God is illustrated for us in the realm of giving alms and of fasting: physical acts. We see God as One who cares for us in such a way that we do not need to think of tomorrow—how to be fed or how to be clothed, the worries that come to us on the physical level. Our Lord is saying, "If you discover Me and receive Me as your King, you will discover that I am the answer to all your physical needs." He first offers Himself to the nation—and to us—on this level.

> The Sermon on the Mount is one of the most penetrating and incisive messages ever set before human beings.

The Sermon on the Mount is followed by a section on miracles, and in chapters 8 through 12 we witness the physical miracles of the kingdom. These are illustrations of the benefits our Lord can bestow on the level of the physical life. This is not just a demonstration of Hollywood-style special effects and pyrotechnics. In fact, it is amazing how unspectacular these miracles are! There is no spectacular display of lights and fire and quadraphonic sound effects here, but rather a simple, dignified representation of our Lord's power over all forces that affect the body: demons, disease, and death. His authority in this realm is that of King—He is sovereign and supreme.

Following the miracles comes a section of parables of the kingdom, where the rejection of the kingdom is declared in mystery form. It is clear that the nation is going to reject our Lord's offer of Himself as King on this physical level, so a new word appears: woe. In chapter 11, He declares, "Woe to you, Korazin! Woe to you, Bethsaida!" Woe to those who have not believed! He pronounces judgment upon the nation on this level, the level of the physical.

The mysteries of the kingdom are found in chapter 13, where the parables are given with truth embedded within symbols—the parable of the

Sidenotes: The Sermon on the Mount · The Physical Miracles · Parables of the Kingdom

sower and the seeds, the parable of the wheat and the weeds (or "tares"), the parable of the mustard seed, the parable of the yeast, the parable of the great catch of fish. This entire section—Matthew 13:54 through 16:20—has to do with bread. There is the feeding of the five thousand in chapter 14; the questions about what defiles a person in chapter 15; the incident of the Canaanite woman who came and asked Jesus to heal her daughter, comparing her request to begging for crumbs from His table; the feeding of the four thousand in chapter 15; and the leaven of the Pharisees and Sadducees in chapter 16.

Finally, in 16:13–20, we encounter the revelation of our Lord's person to Peter at that wonderful moment when Peter is given the first insight into the true nature of his friend, Jesus:

> Simon Peter answered, "You are the Christ, the Son of the living God."
> Jesus replied, "Blessed are you, Simon son of Jonah, for this was not revealed to you by man, but by my Father in heaven"
> (vv. 16–17).

At this point, our Lord's message takes a significant turn. Here is the transition point where Jesus moves beyond the physical, bodily level of our humanity and begins to penetrate to the depths of the human soul.

Israel Is Tested in the Realm of the Soul

The previous section—Israel's testing in the physical realm—was composed of a narrative passage detailing Jesus' ministry, followed by a group of His parables. This section is structured the same way—a narrative of the Lord's ministry, followed by His parables.

Beginning with 16:21, we see the second ministry of our Lord to the nation, this time offering Himself to Israel on the level of the soul. His first revelation (16:21–18:35) is to the disciples only, for they are the nucleus of the coming church. Here is the transfiguration and the first intimation of His death.

Parables of the King

Next come the parables of the King. These are addressed first to the disciples and then to the nation. All are parables presenting Him as the King who has the right to command and to judge the character of individuals: Are they willing to follow Him? Are they willing to obey Him? Are they willing to let Him mold and shape their character?

Practical Instruction for Everyday Living

In Matthew 18, the Lord gives instruction in how to get along with others, how to love each other, forgive each other, and reconcile with each other. It is a masterpiece of practical instruction for everyday living and healthy relationships, and if we would only practice the principles of Matthew 18 in a faithful way in the church, the entire world would be transformed by our example.

> **[Matthew 18] is a masterpiece of practical instruction for everyday living and healthy relationships.**

In Matthew 19, He teaches about marriage, divorce, sexual ethics and morality, promise keeping, and truthfulness. Again, His instruction is aimed at our souls—and if we would keep His teaching, we would change the world.

"Rejoice greatly, O Daughter of Zion!" wrote the prophet Zechariah. "Shout, Daughter of Jerusalem! See, your king comes to you, righteous and having salvation, gentle and riding on a donkey, on a colt, the foal of a donkey" (Zech. 9:9). The prophecy of Zechariah was fulfilled in the triumphal entry when our Lord entered the city of Jerusalem in exactly that manner, and Matthew 21 presents the story of His triumphal entry into Jerusalem. Triumph soon gives way to judgment, however, as the Lord enters the city and pronounces His judgment on the sins of the nation. He strides into the temple, halts the offerings, and drives out the corrupt money changers.

The Triumphal Entry

In Matthew 23 the word *woe* is pronounced with a regularity and a rhythm like the sound of a whip of punishment: verse 13—"Woe to you, teachers of the law and Pharisees, you hypocrites!" Verse 15—"Woe to you, teachers of the law and Pharisees, you hypocrites!" Verse 16—"Woe to you, blind guides!" Verse 23—"Woe to you, teachers of the law and Pharisees, you hypocrites!" And again in verse 25, verse 27, and verse 29. Throughout this chapter, like the knell of death, the word *woe* rings out again and again.

This is followed by a section of instruction in chapters 24 and 25—the famous Olivet Discourse. This discourse contains the Lord's instructions to the believing remnant on what to do until He comes again. It reveals how world history is going to shape up, what will happen in the intervening years, what forces will be loosed upon the earth, how the forces of darkness will shake, test, and try God's own people. He declares that God's people can stand only in the strength of the Holy Spirit.

The Olivet Discourse

Finally, in chapters 26 through 28, we see the betrayal, trial, agony, and crucifixion of the Lord Jesus Christ. Willingly, He steps into the murky darkness of the valley of the shadow of death. There, alone and forsaken by

His friends, He enters into a death grapple with the powers of darkness. In the mystery of the cross, He lays hold of the forces that have mastered the human spirit and He shatters them there. Amazingly, though the Gospel of Matthew presents Jesus as King, the only crown He ever wears in His earthly life is a crown of thorns; the only throne He ever mounts is a bloody cross; the only scepter He ever wields is a broken reed.

Israel Is Tested in the Realm of the Spirit

What follows the crucifixion is an event so astounding, so shattering, that it represents a complete historical break with all that has gone before: The resurrection of Jesus Christ. At the moment of Jesus' resurrection, He broke through into the realm of the human spirit; the very center of humanity's being was opened wide. As we come to know the Lord in our spirits, we discover that the worship of our hearts is given to Him there. The spirit is the key to the mastery of an entire human life.

> **The spirit is the key to the mastery of an entire human life.**

When you get a person's spirit, you have all that he or she is. By means of the cross and the resurrection, our Lord made it possible to pass into the very Holy of Holies of our humanity—the spirit—so that God could make His dwelling place within us.

The great message of the Gospel, then, is that God is not out there, way up yonder, somewhere beyond the blue. He is not waiting in some distant judgment hall to impose His condemnation on us. He is ready and waiting to pass right into the center of a hungry, thirsty person's heart and to pour out His blessing, His character, His being, His life into that life. When the King is enthroned in a human life, the kingdom of God is present on earth. That is the message of Matthew: Repent, for the kingdom of heaven is at hand. Heaven is not someplace far out in space; it is here among us, invisible yet utterly real in the life of one where God reigns in the spirit. Where the King is, there is the kingdom. If King Jesus is enthroned in the heart, the kingdom of God has come.

> **If King Jesus is enthroned in the heart, the kingdom of God has come.**

The Gospel of Matthew challenges us with the most crucial and personal question facing every human being: "Is Jesus Christ King of your life?" A king is more than a savior; a king is a sovereign. King Jesus demands every corner of our lives. If we have received Jesus as the Savior of only our physical beings or the Savior of our souls, then we have not yet made Him

King. He must penetrate, invade, and conquer every square inch of our lives, even the deep places of the spirit.

Has Jesus penetrated your spirit and mastered your heart? Is He the single most important person in all the universe to you? Until you meet Him and receive Him as King, you have not truly met Jesus.

May you and I respond in obedience to the message of Matthew. May we truly behold—and surrender to—our King. And may we cast out the throne of our own ego, self-will, and pride, replacing it with the bloody, glorious throne of Jesus, the cross of Calvary. Then His rule in our lives will be complete—body, soul, and spirit.

NOTES

NOTES

NOTES

NOTES

NOTES

NOTES

ADVENTURING
through the
LIFE *of* CHRIST

CHAPTER THREE

MARK:
HE CAME
to SERVE

ONE OF THE GREATEST LEADERS of the twentieth century went about barefoot, wearing the simple clothing of the poor, traveling either on foot or in the cheapest railway class. He never lived in a palace or mansion, but chose to make his home in the slums among the poor people he loved. His name was Mohandas Karamchand "Mahatma" Gandhi, and he led a nonviolent struggle to shake off British rule and bring self-government to the people of India. He was a moral and political leader—yet he led not by political power but by an example of humble servanthood. Though he was of the Hindu religion, he studied the life of Jesus and patterned his actions after the servanthood model of Jesus.

In 1931, Gandhi went to several European nations to visit the leaders of various states. Wherever he went, he took a goat with him as a symbol of his own lowliness and humility. When he went to Rome to pay a call on the Italian dictator Mussolini, he arrived, as always, dressed in old beggar's clothes, leading his goat by a rope. Mussolini's children laughed when they saw the thin, bald, powerless-looking man—but the dictator snapped at them and ordered them to be silent. "That scrawny old man and his scrawny old goat," he said, "are shaking the British Empire."

The Power of a True Servant

That is the power of a true servant: the power to shake kingdoms, the power that was first modeled for us by the greatest servant of all, Jesus Christ, the Servant-Lord.

The Gospel of Mark, the second book in the New Testament, is the briefest of the four Gospels, only sixteen chapters long. It is easily read in a single sitting. Its brevity is probably the reason it is the most-often-translated book of the New Testament. The Wycliffe translators usually begin their translation work with Mark's Gospel because it so succinctly gives the whole Gospel story.

The Author of Mark

The writer of the Gospel of Mark was a young man named John Mark, who accompanied Paul on his first missionary journey and proved to be a less-than-dependable servant. He could not take the pressure and turned back to go home. Interestingly, the Holy Spirit chose this man, who had shown qualities of unreliability early in his career, to record for us the absolute dependability, reliability, and faithfulness of the Servant of God, the Lord Jesus Christ.

Mark was a companion of Peter, who was one of the Lord's closest friends in His earthly ministry, so the Gospel of Mark contains many of the thoughts, teachings, and firsthand impressions of Peter. Of the four

Gospel writers, Matthew and John were disciples of Jesus Christ, Luke received his Gospel through the teaching of the apostle Paul, and Mark received his Gospel at the feet of Peter—and though Peter wrote two New Testament letters, he did not write a Gospel account.

> **Mark was a companion of Peter, who was one of the Lord's closest friends in His earthly ministry.**

In Acts 10, Peter gives a brief summary of all that is recorded for us in the Gospel of Mark. In the home of Cornelius, Peter stood and told the people "how God anointed Jesus of Nazareth with the Holy Spirit and power, and how he went around doing good and healing all who were under the power of the devil, because God was with him" (10:38).

If you would like to meet Mark personally, turn to Mark 14. There, in the account of Jesus' capture in the Garden of Gethsemane, just before the crucifixion, we find the only account of Mark's appearance among the disciples. In verses 51–52 we read:

> *A young man, wearing nothing but a linen garment, was following Jesus. When they seized him, he fled naked, leaving his garment behind.*

No other Gospel tells us that, and it is almost certain that this young man is Mark. He was the son of a rich woman in Jerusalem and it is very likely that his mother owned the house in which the disciples met in the Upper Room. Mark, therefore, was present at some of these events. Most Bible scholars are convinced that this incident is included in Mark's Gospel because he himself was involved.

The Outline of Mark, the Gospel of the Servant

The whole Gospel of Mark is summed up in a phrase from Mark 10:45: "Even the Son of Man did not come to be served, but to serve." Or, as the King James Version puts it, "not to be ministered unto, but to minister." In this short verse, you have the outline of the Gospel of Mark, because the concluding phrase of this verse goes on to say, "and to give his life as a ransom for many." From Mark 1:1 to 8:30, the theme of this book is the ministry of the Servant, Christ. From 8:31 to the end of the book, the theme is the ransoming work of the Servant.

The Ministry of the Servant (Mark 1:1–8:30)

1. The credentials of the Servant: John   1:1–11
    the Baptist announces and baptizes Jesus
2. The testing of the Servant: temptation   1:12–13
    in the wilderness
3. The ministry of the Servant: 1:14–2:12
    miracles, healings, authority over
    demons and disease
4. Controversy and opposition over Jesus'   2:13–3:35
    friendship with sinners, work on
    the Sabbath
5. Four parables of the Servant: 4:1–34
    the soils, the lamp, the growing seed,
    the mustard seed
6. Four Servant miracles: the sea is stilled,   4:35–5:43
    demons cast into pigs, the raising of
    Jairus's daughter, the healing of the
    woman with a flow of blood
7. Increasing opposition to the Servant   6:1–8:21
    and the death of John the Baptist
8. The healing of the blind man   8:22–26
    from Bethsaida
9. Peter's confession of Christ   8:27–30

The Ransoming Work of the Servant (Mark 8:31–16:20)

10. Jesus begins teaching about   8:31–8:38
    His impending death
11. Jesus is transfigured on the mountain   9:1–13
12. Jesus delivers a demon-possessed son   9:14–29
13. Jesus prepares His disciples for His death   9:30–32
14. Teachings on servanthood; death and   9:33–10:31
    hell; marriage and divorce; children;
    wealth; and the eternal reward, including
    the story of the rich young ruler
15. Jesus again predicts His death and   10:32–45
    teaches servanthood
16. Blind Bartimaeus is healed   10:46–52

In the first half of the book, from 1:1 to 8:30, two aspects of the Servant's ministry are stressed: His authority and His effect on people. Notice first the signs of His authority.

The Authority of the Servant

Those who listened to Jesus were filled with astonishment. They said, in effect, "He doesn't teach like the scribes and Pharisees, but He speaks with authority and with power. What He says to us pierces our hearts like a power drill!"

Why did Jesus speak with such authority? Because, as the Servant of God, He knew the secrets of God. He reached into the treasury of God and drew out the secrets of God; then He made those rich secrets known to human beings. Since we are human beings, we hear His words with a sense of awareness that this is reality—ultimate reality. There is a note of genuineness about what He says, and that ring of truth has the power to stop us dead in our tracks, to convict us of our sin and our need of Him. That is why the Gospels and the words of our Lord, as they are read, have power in themselves to convict human beings.

The scribes and Pharisees needed constantly to bolster themselves with references to authorities and quotations from others, but not our Lord. He never quotes anything but the Scriptures. He always speaks with the final word of authority. He never apologizes, never ventures a mere opinion, never hesitates or equivocates. He speaks always with utter authority—the same authority that once said, "Let there be light," and there was light.

In this section, His authority over the powers of darkness—the demon world—is underscored. It is a world that we take all too casually. A prime example of how seriously we underestimate the powers of darkness is our observance of a holiday called Halloween. With Halloween, we show our dim and inadequate awareness of the existence of evil spirits. We celebrate

Power to Convict Human Beings

Authority Over the Powers of Darkness

the day as an amused tribute to a pantheon of goblins, spooks, and witches on broomsticks—a distortion of the true nature of evil that has succeeded in dulling our sensitivity to the reality of the spiritual world—and the realm of ultimate evil. Behind this clownish facade of Halloween is a real and deadly world of demonic power that controls human minds and influences human events.

As you read through the Gospel of Mark, you see again and again the authority of the Servant of God over the mysterious forces of darkness. The world of the occult is wide open to Him. He knows the black powers, the dark passions that work behind the scenes of history. Paul calls these demonic powers "seducing spirits" or "deceiving spirits" (see 1 Tim. 4:1). Jesus has ultimate authority over those powers, but they can do us great harm if we fail to place ourselves under the protective umbrella of His lordship.

> Jesus has ultimate authority over those powers, but they can do us great harm if we fail to place ourselves under the protective umbrella of His lordship.

As you read the Gospel of Mark, you see that these demonic powers influence people to do strange things—to isolate themselves in the wilderness away from the rest of humanity, to behave in lawless ways (lawlessness is always a mark of demonic influence), to torment themselves and attack others, to menace society. Mark describes one demon-possessed man as "beside himself" (see Mark 3:21 KJV; in the NIV this verse says, "He is out of his mind"). Now, that is a significant phrase, isn't it? Imagine standing beside yourself—a split personality, alienated from your own self. That is one of the marks of demonic influence. And despite the immense power and menace of demonic powers, the Lord Jesus has complete authority and power over them all.

Authority Over Disease

Mark also reveals the power of Christ the Servant over disease. The first account of that power at work is the healing of Peter's mother-in-law. That has always been a touching scene for me. People today often joke about mothers-in-law, but Peter was evidently very concerned and loving toward his wife's mother. Our Lord touched her, and her fever left her. Then all the people of the city gathered about His door, and He healed every one of them (see 1:30–34).

The next account is that of a leper (1:40–45). Jesus did the unheard-of thing: He not only healed the leper, but He touched him. No one ever touched a leper in those days. The Law of Moses (which was, in many ways, a law of health and hygiene as much as a law of morality) forbade that lepers be touched, and the lepers had to go about calling a warning—"Unclean! Unclean!" No one would remotely think of touching a leper, but the compassion of the Servant's heart is revealed in this story as Jesus touches the leper, heals him, and sends him to the priest. This is the first instance in all of Scripture of a leper's ever being healed according to the Law of Moses and sent to the priest, as the Law demanded.

The Servant's Effect on People

A second major emphasis of Mark's Gospel focuses on the powerful effect Jesus had on the people with whom He came in contact. A servant is always affecting people, and as Jesus the Servant performed His ministry and went about doing good, people responded to Him—and those responses were always strongly favorable or strongly unfavorable. Jesus is not the sort of person you can ignore or treat with indifference. He either inspires your devotion—or your hatred.

> **Jesus is not the sort of person you can ignore or treat with indifference.**

We see His effect on His own disciples after He, first, feeds the five *His Disciples* thousand, then amazes them by walking on the water and calming the storm on the sea. In 6:51–52, we read:

> *Then he climbed into the boat with them, and the wind died down. They were completely amazed, for they had not understood about the loaves; their hearts were hardened.*

This hardening of the heart is characteristic of the attitudes of many toward our Lord in His ministry as a servant.

In chapter 7, we encounter the hypocrisy and criticism of the Pharisees, *The Pharisees* but also the astonished acceptance of many who were deeply affected after seeing Jesus' miracles of healing:

> *People were overwhelmed with amazement. "He has done everything well," they said. "He even makes the deaf hear and the mute speak" (7:37).*

That is the mark of a believing heart, the heart of one who can say of *The Common* Jesus, "He does all things well." *People*

Mark 8:22–26 goes on to record a very significant act of our Lord:

*They came to Bethsaida, and some people brought a blind man
and begged Jesus to touch him. He took the blind man by the hand
and led him outside the village. When he had spit on the man's
eyes and put his hands on him, Jesus asked, "Do you see anything?"*

*He looked up and said, "I see people; they look like trees walk-
ing around."*

*Once more Jesus put his hands on the man's eyes. Then his eyes
were opened, his sight was restored, and he saw everything clearly.
Jesus sent him home, saying, "Don't go into the village."*

Notice that this story is set in the village of Bethsaida. Matthew
describes Bethsaida as one of those places Jesus had pronounced judgment upon, saying,

*"Woe to you, Korazin! Woe to you, Bethsaida! If the miracles that were
performed in you had been performed in Tyre and Sidon, they would
have repented long ago in sackcloth and ashes" (Matthew 11:21).*

Here is a village that had rejected our Lord's ministry and His person,
and He would not allow any further testimony to go on in that place. He
led the blind man out of the village before He healed him. (This is the
only instance where our Lord did not see an instantaneous, complete healing take place the first time He spoke.) When the healing was complete,
He would not even allow the healed man to go back into the village, for
Bethsaida was under God's judgment for having rejected the ministry of
the Servant of God.

In 8:27–33, we find the story of Peter's confession that Jesus is the
Christ, the Messiah whose coming was prophesied in the Old Testament.
This incident ends the first part of the Gospel of Mark.

The Ransoming Servant

Beginning with the second part of the book, at Mark 8:34, we come
to the second great theme of the Gospel of Mark: that Jesus came to give
His life a ransom for many. Here, Jesus increasingly begins to instruct His
disciples regarding His impending death upon the cross—the ransoming
ministry of the Servant—and He introduces this somber theme as He
begins to instruct His disciples regarding His death:

He then began to teach them that the Son of Man must suffer many things and be rejected by the elders, chief priests and teachers of the law, and that he must be killed and after three days rise again. He spoke plainly about this, and Peter took him aside and began to rebuke him.

But when Jesus turned and looked at his disciples, he rebuked Peter. "Get behind me, Satan!" he said. "You do not have in mind the things of God, but the things of men" (8:31–33).

From this point on, our Lord's face is set toward Jerusalem and the cross. He is going now to be the offering of God—the Servant who gives Himself completely as a sacrificial ransom for those He came to save and to serve. The revelation of His plan is given in this passage: He came to suffer, to be rejected, to be killed, and after three days, to rise again.

> **Our Lord's face is set toward Jerusalem and the cross.**

And who stood up to thwart that plan? Not Judas Iscariot! Not Pontius Pilate! Not some demonic spirit! No, it was Jesus' close, trusted friend, Peter, the one who had just confessed that Jesus is the Christ, the Messiah! His response to Jesus was, "Don't sacrifice yourself, Lord! Spare yourself!" That is always the way of fallen humanity. The philosophy of the world is, "Spare yourself. Serve yourself. Don't do anything you don't have to." That's the dominant philosophy of our age!

But Jesus rebuked him. "Peter," He said, in effect, "I recognize where that comes from. That is the wisdom of Satan, not God. Get that kind of talk out of My way."

Then Jesus called the multitude to Him, along with His disciples, and said to them, "If anyone would come after me, he must deny himself and take up his cross and follow me" (8:34). Sparing yourself, seeking yourself, indulging yourself is the way of the devil. Giving yourself is the way of God. This is the plan that Christ carries through to the end of Mark's Gospel—a plan of giving Himself away in a sacrificial ransom for you and for me.

The account of the transfiguration follows in chapter 9. There, Jesus reveals His intention and His purpose: The Transfiguration

He said to them, "I tell you the truth, some who are standing here will not taste death before they see the kingdom of God come with power."

> *After six days Jesus took Peter, James and John with him and led them up a high mountain, where they were all alone. There he was transfigured before them. His clothes became dazzling white, whiter than anyone in the world could bleach them. And there appeared before them Elijah and Moses, who were talking with Jesus.*
>
> *Peter said to Jesus, "Rabbi, it is good for us to be here. Let us put up three shelters—one for you, one for Moses and one for Elijah." (He did not know what to say, they were so frightened.)*
>
> *Then a cloud appeared and enveloped them, and a voice came from the cloud: "This is my Son, whom I love. Listen to him!"*
>
> *Suddenly, when they looked around, they no longer saw anyone with them except Jesus (9:1–8).*

Jesus led Peter, James, and John up on the mountaintop, and there—as Jesus promised—they saw "the kingdom of God come with power." They didn't have to go through death to see the glory of the King—they saw it with their own earthly, mortal eyes. Peter refers to this event in his second letter:

> *We did not follow cleverly invented stories when we told you about the power and coming of our Lord Jesus Christ, but we were eye-witnesses of his majesty. For he received honor and glory from God the Father when the voice came to him from the Majestic Glory, saying, "This is my Son, whom I love; with him I am well pleased." We ourselves heard this voice that came from heaven when we were with him on the sacred mountain. (2 Peter 1:16–18).*

Why did Jesus preface this incident with the statement, "Some who are standing here will not taste death before they see the kingdom of God come with power"? Because His intention for the human race, the very purpose of His redemptive work, is that human beings should not have to taste death. He came to deliver us from the awful sting of death. Christians die, but they never taste death. Death is a doorway into life. Why can the apostle Paul say with such confidence, "Where, O death, is your victory? Where, O death, is your sting?" (1 Cor. 15:55)? Because, as Hebrews 2:9 tells us, Jesus tasted death for everyone, for you and for me, so that we don't have to.

The disciples didn't understand the Lord's purpose or His words regarding life and death. In Mark 9:9–10, we read:

*As they were coming down the mountain, Jesus gave them orders
not to tell anyone what they had seen until the Son of Man had
risen from the dead. They kept the matter to themselves, discussing
what "rising from the dead" meant.*

What does "rising from the dead" mean? It means just what it says!
Jesus couldn't have spoken any more plainly. He was going to suffer, He
was going to die, He was going to rise and live again. The disciples were
looking for figures of speech when Jesus was giving them literal, plain,
practical truth.

In chapter 10, Jesus speaks of the family, of the children, of God's material and monetary blessings. He goes into the junkyard of human life and
takes these gifts of God that people have twisted and selfishly misused—
and He beautifully restores them to the purpose God intended.

The Last Week

In chapter 11, we have the beginning of our Lord's last week as He
moves resolutely toward His rendezvous with the cross. In this chapter, we
see another significant act that only Mark records:

*On reaching Jerusalem, Jesus entered the temple area and began
driving out those who were buying and selling there. He overturned
the tables of the money changers and the benches of those selling
doves, and would not allow anyone to carry merchandise through
the temple courts. And as he taught them, he said, "Is it not written:
" 'My house will be called a house of prayer for all nations'? But
you have made it 'a den of robbers' " (11:15–17).*

Now, this is not the same cleansing of the temple recorded by John in
his Gospel (John 2:13–16). In John's Gospel, this incident occurred at
the beginning of our Lord's ministry. But now, at the end of His ministry,
for the second time, He overthrows the tables of the money changers and
cleanses the temple.

From the temple, Jesus moves out to the Mount of Olives, from there to
the Upper Room, then into the Garden of Gethsemane, and on to the cross.

The last chapters of Mark's Gospel are concerned with the questions that
people asked Jesus. In chapter 11, He answers the questions of the priests
and the elders who approached Him with hatred and tried to trap Him with
their questions. In chapter 12, He answers the questions of the Pharisees

and the Herodians who likewise tried to trap Him with their questions. Also in chapter 12, the Sadducees tried to trap Him (they were the materialists, the ones who did not believe in a resurrection or a spirit life).

Finally, a scribe with an honest heart asked Him the only honest question recorded in these chapters: "Of all the commandments, which is the most important?" (12:28). Immediately and forthrightly our Lord answered him:

> "The most important one," answered Jesus, "is this: 'Hear, O Israel, the Lord our God, the Lord is one. Love the Lord your God with all your heart and with all your soul and with all your mind and with all your strength.' The second is this: 'Love your neighbor as yourself.' There is no commandment greater than these."
>
> "Well said, teacher," the man replied. "You are right in saying that God is one and there is no other but him. To love him with all your heart, with all your understanding and with all your strength, and to love your neighbor as yourself is more important than all burnt offerings and sacrifices."
>
> When Jesus saw that he had answered wisely, he said to him, "You are not far from the kingdom of God." And from then on no one dared ask him any more questions (12:29–34).

Jesus stopped all questions. That is the power of truth—it elevates the honest heart, it shames the guilty heart, it silences the lying tongue.

In chapter 13, the disciples come to Jesus asking about future events. Here our Lord unfolds the whole revelation of the age to come—the time of tribulation and the time of His return in glory.

> That is the power of truth—it elevates the honest heart, it shames the guilty heart, it silences the lying tongue.

Chapter 14 describes two acts that contrast sharply. First, a woman named Mary offers her sacrifice of expensive perfume, which she pours out on Jesus' feet. Next, Judas Iscariot betrays his Lord for money. One is an act of utter selflessness, and the other an act of complete selfishness.

Beginning with chapter 15, we find the account of the cross. In Mark's account this is an act of almost incredible brutality done in the name of justice. The Lord outwardly seems to be a defeated man, a tragic failure, His cause hopelessly lost. He is ridiculed, beaten, and spat upon. As He Himself said, "The Son of Man must suffer many things" (8:31).

The Death and Resurrection of the Servant

Finally, the Servant goes willingly to the cross and is crucified. It seems so unlike the picture of the wonder-worker of Galilee who begins this Gospel—the mighty person of power, the Servant with authority from on high. No wonder the high priests, as they saw Him hanging there, said of Him, "He saved others, but he can't save himself!" (Mark 15:31). That is a strange statement. Yet it is one of those remarkable statements that reveal how God is able to make even His enemies praise Him, because they were, paradoxically, both right and wrong. They were wrong in the sense that they were mocking His seeming helplessness; they were right in that Jesus did save others by the very act of refusing to save Himself!

As I read this account, I am impressed with the three things that they could not make our Lord do. First, they could not make Him speak: They could not make Him speak.

Again Pilate asked him, "Aren't you going to answer? See how many things they are accusing you of."
But Jesus still made no reply, and Pilate was amazed (15:4–5).

Why didn't He speak? Because He would have saved Himself if He had spoken before Pilate. The high priests were right: He saved others, but Himself He could not—would not—save.

Second, they could not make Him drink: They could not make Him drink.

They offered him wine mixed with myrrh, but he did not take it (15:23).

Why not? Well, because He could have saved Himself if He had. The wine and myrrh were a narcotic mixture to dull the senses. Had He drunk, He would have saved Himself the full effect of the agony of the cross and the weight of the sin and pain of the world coming upon His shoulders, but He would not. He would not spare Himself.

Finally, they could not even make Him die. In the NIV we read, "With a loud cry, Jesus breathed his last" (Mark 15:37), which is not literally what the original Greek text conveys. In the Greek, this verse reads, "With a loud cry, Jesus unspirited Himself." He dismissed His spirit. He didn't die at the hands of the murderers; He let His spirit go of His own free will. Jesus Himself had said, They could not make Him die.

> *"I lay down my life—only to take it up again. No one takes it from me, but I lay it down of my own accord. I have authority to lay it down and authority to take it up again. This command I received from my Father" (John 10:17–18).*

Jesus could have refused to die, and the soldiers, the rulers, and the religious leaders could not have taken His life from Him. He could have even hung on the cross and taunted them with their inability to put Him to death, but He did not. He died, He unspirited Himself, willingly and deliberately.

When we come to the final chapter of Mark, the resurrection, we learn why our Lord did not allow these three things.

He was silent and refused to appeal to Pilate or the crowd because He was laying the basis for a coming day when in resurrection power He would appeal to a far greater crowd, when every knee should bow and every tongue should proclaim that Jesus Christ is Lord to the glory of God the Father.

He would not drink to dull His senses because He was laying a basis upon which even those who stood about the cross might enter into a life so wonderful, so abundant, that the most thrilling and emotionally intense moments of life on earth would pale by comparison.

Finally, He would not let human beings take His life because He needed to voluntarily lay it down Himself so that He might overcome humanity's greatest enemy—death—and forever deliver all who would believe in Him from the power and the sting of death. That is the gospel. He saved others, but Himself He could not—would not—save. That is the attitude of the True Servant (see Phil. 2:5–7).

As we study the life of the greatest Servant who ever lived, as we seek to pattern our lives after His, may we always bear upon our lives the selfless, sacrificial imprint of the One who, by refusing to save Himself, saved others—saved me and saved you.

NOTES

NOTES

NOTES

NOTES

NOTES

ADVENTURING
through the
LIFE *of* CHRIST

CHAPTER FOUR

LUKE:
THE PERFECT
MAN

K ING CANUTE, the Danish king of England in the eleventh century, was surrounded by a court of fawning, flattering yes-men. "O King Canute," they said, "you are the greatest, most powerful king who ever lived! You are invincible! There is nothing you do not know! You are perfection incarnate!"

A humble and realistic man, King Canute soon tired of all this empty praise. So, he commanded his palace guard to lift his throne off the dais in the throne room and carry it to the seashore. The king and all of his fawning (and, now, very perplexed) yes-men followed the throne all the way to the seashore. There King Canute commanded that the throne be set down in the sand at the water's edge. The yes-men gathered around wondering what the king had in mind.

King Canute settled himself onto his throne, looking out to sea. He stretched out his arms and commanded, "Waves, be still! Tide, be stopped!" But the waves continued to roll in to the shore, and the tide continued to rise. The sea came up around King Canute's ankles, then his thighs, then his chest. Yet he continued to command, "Waves, be still! Tide, be stopped!" Finally, a wave came crashing in that toppled the throne and cast King Canute up on the sand, gasping and sputtering.

Wide-eyed, the yes-men stared at the king whom they had called perfection incarnate, believing that he had completely lost his mind. The king stood up, wringing wet, and ordered his throne carried back to the castle. The entire entourage trudged back home. Arriving once more in the throne room, King Canute led the group of yes-men to a large carved crucifix, a statue of Jesus upon the cross. "Do you all see this man? He did what I cannot do! He stilled the waves, He commanded the sea! He is perfection incarnate. I am just a man."

Then he removed his golden crown and placed it on the brow of the statue of Jesus. The crown remained on that statue until Canute's death.

The Gospel of Luke is the Gospel of the man who was perfection incarnate, the only truly perfect human being.

The Structure of Luke

The third Gospel presents Jesus as the Son of Man. That was our Lord's favorite title for Himself—a title He used more frequently than any other name. As you read the Gospel of Luke, you meet the same person you meet in Matthew, Mark, and John. But note the difference in emphases among the four Gospels. In Matthew, the emphasis is upon Jesus' kingliness; in Mark, the emphasis is on His servanthood; in John, the emphasis is on His deity. But here in Luke, the emphasis is on His humanity.

The essential manhood and humanity of Christ are continually underscored throughout this Gospel. The key to the Gospel is found in Luke 19:10. In fact, this verse sets forth a handy outline of the entire book:

> *"The Son of Man came to seek and to save what was lost."*

The "Son of Man" was our Lord's favorite title for Himself—a title He used more frequently than any other name.

In that one sentence we find the structure and divisions of this Gospel.

First section: "The Son of Man came." In the beginning of this Gospel, from 1:1 to 4:13, Luke tells us how Jesus entered the human race, including His genealogy.

Second section: "to seek." The Lord's earthly ministry consisted largely of seeking people out and moving into the heart of humanity, penetrating deeply into human emotions, thoughts, and feelings. In the middle section of Luke, from 4:14 through 19:27, Jesus carries on His ministry among people, putting His finger on the throbbing centers of their pain, shame, and motivations, and touching their humanity with His healing power. This section climaxes with His journey to Jerusalem, the place where He will be sacrificed, as we read in Luke 9:51:

> *As the time approached for him to be taken up to heaven, Jesus resolutely set out for Jerusalem.*

The record of His journey to Jerusalem occupies chapters 9 through 19 and recounts a number of important incidents along the way.

Third section: "and to save what was lost." Here the Lord moves into the final act of the drama of His life: to save humanity by means of the cross and the resurrection. In Luke 19:28, we read:

> *After Jesus had said this, he went on ahead, going up to Jerusalem.*

This verse marks the close of Jesus' seeking ministry and the beginning of His saving ministry. It introduces the last section of the book, in which He enters the city, goes to the temple, ascends the Mount of Olives, is taken to Pilate's judgment hall, and then to the cross, to the tomb, and to resurrection day.

The Outline of Luke, the Gospel of the Son of Man

The Coming of the Son of Man (Luke 1:1–4:13)

1. Introduction: The purpose of Luke's Gospel   1:1–4
2. Events leading up to the birth of Christ   1:5–56
3. The birth of John the Baptist   1:57–80
4. The birth of Jesus Christ   2:1–38
5. The childhood of Jesus Christ   2:39–52
6. The ministry of John the Baptist   3:1–20
7. The baptism of Jesus by John the Baptist   3:21–22
8. The genealogy of the Son of Man   3:23–38
9. The temptation of the Son of Man   4:1–13

His Ministry—The Son of Man Seeks (Luke 4:14–19:27)

10. The beginning of His ministry, His acceptance in Galilee, His rejection in His hometown   4:14–30
11. Miracles demonstrating His power over demons, sickness, and paralysis; also, His calling of the first disciples   4:31–5:28
12. Jesus and the Pharisees   5:29–6:11
13. Jesus instructs the disciples, the Beatitudes, the Christian way of life, parables   6:12–49
14. Miracles, the healing of the centurion's son, the raising of the widow's son   7:1–16
15. Jesus praises John the Baptist   7:17–35
16. Jesus dines at a Pharisee's home, a woman anoints His feet with costly perfume   7:36–50
17. Parables and miracles, the storm is stilled, demons are cast into swine, a woman with an issue of blood is healed, Jairus's daughter is raised   8
18. The Twelve are sent to preach   9:1–11
19. Jesus feeds the five thousand   9:12–17
20. Peter's confession of faith   9:18–26

His Death and Resurrection—The Son of Man Saves (Luke 19:28–24:53)

The Lost Secret of Humanity

Notice the exact words Jesus uses in the key passage of Luke 19:10: "to save what was lost." He is not talking only about coming to save lost people. He has come to save what was lost.

What was lost? Not just people themselves, but the essence of what people were created to be. Jesus came to save and restore our God-given humanity, which was created in the image of God. That is the secret of our humanity. We have forgotten what we were intended to be at Creation. The whole dilemma of life is that we still have, deep within us, a kind of racial memory of what we ought to be, what we want to be, what we were made to be—but we don't know how to accomplish it. The secret of our humanity was lost long ago.

A group of scientists once met at Princeton University to discuss the latest findings in astronomy. One distinguished astronomer stood and said, "When you consider the vast distances between the stars in a single galaxy, then consider the even greater distances between the various galaxies, then consider the fact that the galaxies themselves are arranged in clusters, and the clusters of galaxies are separated by even more enormous distances, we astronomers have to conclude that man is nothing more than an insignificant dot in the infinite universe."

Just then, a familiar stooped figure rose up, his head fringed with an unruly white mane, his frayed sweater bunched up around his thin frame. "Insignificant, you say?" said Professor Einstein. "Yes, I have often felt that man is an insignificant dot in the universe—but then I recalled that the same insignificant dot who is man . . . is also the astronomer."

That is the essence of humanity; that is the greatness that God created within us when He made us in His image. Yes, the universe is vast and we are small—but we are not insignificant. God has created us to seek answers and understanding of the vast questions and issues of the cosmos. There is something unaccountably grand about human beings, some hidden specialness that God placed inside us—something that was marred and distorted by sin but that still glimmers within us. It is this wonderful lost secret, this glorious and impenetrable lost mystery, which our Lord came to restore and to save, that we discover in the Gospel of Luke.

> The universe is vast and we are small—but we are not insignificant.

The Author of Luke

The author of this Gospel is Luke, the physician, the companion and loyal friend of Paul. Luke, himself a Greek, writes to Theophilus, also a Greek. We know little about Theophilus, but he was evidently a friend of Luke (see Luke 1:1–4) who had become acquainted with the Christian faith, and Luke now attempts to explain it more fully to him. It is most interesting and fitting that Luke should be the one to write this Gospel that deals with the humanity of our Lord, for the ideal of the Greek was the perfection of humanity—an ideal that Jesus fulfilled.

> The ideal of the Greek was the perfection of humanity—an ideal that Jesus fulfilled.

We cannot read the Gospel of Luke thoughtfully without noting some remarkable similarities between it and the epistle to the Hebrews. Therefore, I believe (though it cannot be proven) that Luke wrote the epistle to the Hebrews. I believe Paul authored the thoughts of Hebrews, and that he probably wrote these thoughts in the Hebrew language and sent them to the Jews of Jerusalem. Then Luke, wanting to make these same marvelous truths available to the Gentile world, translated them from Hebrew into Greek, partially paraphrasing rather than actually translating, so that many of his own expressions are found in the epistle. Scholars recognize the thoughts of Hebrews as being very much like Paul's, but the words and manner of expression in the Greek appear to be Luke's. If that is true, then we have

Luke and the
Epistle to the
Hebrews

an explanation for some of the remarkable parallels between Hebrews and the Gospel of Luke.

The amazing message of Hebrews is that Jesus Christ became a human being so He could enter the human condition and become our representative. Hebrews is built around the symbolism of the old covenant and especially the tabernacle in the wilderness, and this epistle explains the meaning of God's symbolic picture of the tabernacle. When Moses went up onto the mountain, he was given a pattern to follow explicitly in making the tabernacle, a pattern of heavenly realities that our human senses cannot perceive.

As you read Hebrews, you discover that the tabernacle was a remarkable picture of humanity. The tabernacle was built in three sections: the outer court, which even the Gentiles could enter; the Holy Place, which was restricted; and the Holy of Holies, which was highly restricted. The sacrifices were offered in the outer court. The priest took the blood and carried it into the Holy Place, where it was sprinkled on the altar. But once a year, the high priest, only under the most precise conditions, was allowed to enter behind the veil into the Holy of Holies. Apart from that single time each year, no one was permitted to enter the Holy of Holies on pain of death, for the mystery of the Shekinah, the presence of God, lived in that sacred, awesome place.

What does all this mean? It is a picture of our humanity in our fallen state. We are that tabernacle in which God planned from the beginning to dwell.

We have an outer court—the body, which is made of the earth and puts us in touch with the earth and the material life around us.

We have a Holy Place—the soul, the place of intimacy, the seat of the mind, the conscience, the memory, and other mysterious inner aspects of our humanity. It is our souls—what the Greek New Testament calls the psuche (or psyche)—that are the part of us studied by psychology and psychiatry.

We have a Holy of Holies—that which is behind the veil and impenetrable. We cannot enter there. We know that something more, something deeper, is hidden in the soulish aspects of our lives. This hidden dimension of our beings is the place where God intended to dwell—the very core of our human existence—the human spirit. Because it is largely inoperative in fallen humanity, people tend to act like intelligent animals. Hidden beneath our bodies and our

> We know that something more, something deeper, is hidden in the soulish aspects of our lives.

souls, the spirit cannot be observed or studied, but it is real and it is the place where God wishes to live among us—the ultimate dwelling place of His Shekinah glory.

In the Gospel of Luke we trace the coming of the one who at last penetrates into that secret place, who enters the mysterious human spirit and rends the veil, so that human beings might discover the mystery of their innermost selves—and find complete joy, peace, and fulfillment. That is what people everywhere desperately look for.

There is nothing more exciting than a sense of fulfillment, of achieving the full possibilities of our personalities. We all seek it—but we have lost the key. Until that key is placed in our hands again by the Son of Man, our full possibilities remain lost.

Jesus came to seek and to save that which was lost within us. That is the good news of Luke.

The Lord's Entrance

The body represents the outer court, and in Luke 1:1–4:13 we see the Lord, the Son of Man, coming into the outer court of our humanity by becoming a human being with a human body. Luke records three facts about Jesus' entrance into our world, our outer court:

First fact: His virgin birth. Some people openly deny the Virgin Birth; some even stand in pulpits declaring that this fact of Jesus' entrance into our world is really unimportant and unhistorical. But it is supremely important. Luke (who was a doctor and, as such, put his physician's seal of approval on this remarkable biological mystery) tells us that a human being was born of a virgin. Mary had a son, and His name was Jesus. The wonder of that mystery is given in the simple, artlessly told story that Luke presents to us.

Furthermore, Jesus' birth is rooted in history by means of a human genealogy. It is important to note the difference between Luke's genealogy and Matthew's. Matthew, the Gospel of the King, traces Jesus' lineage back to King David. Luke, the Gospel of the Son of Man, traces Jesus' lineage all the way back to Adam, the first human being, whom Luke calls "the son of God," since Adam had no earthly father but was directly created by the hand of God. Thus, Luke links the First Adam with the Second Adam (Jesus Christ) in this Gospel of the Son of Man.

Second fact: Our Lord's presentation in the temple at age twelve. Luke tells how Jesus astounded the learned men of the law with His ability to ask probing questions, to answer questions, and to understand deep issues of the Scriptures. Here we see His amazing mental ability and wisdom. Just as His body was perfect and sinless through the Virgin Birth, so His mind and soul (or psyche) are revealed as perfect.

Third fact: The temptation in the wilderness, where the Lord was revealed as being perfect in the innermost recesses of His spirit. This is indicated in advance by the announcement at His baptism, when He is pronounced by the voice of God to be "my Son, whom I love; with you I am well pleased" (3:22). So we have seen Him pass from the outer court of our humanity, to the Holy Place of the soul, to the innermost Holy of Holies of the spirit. He has entered into the very center of our being, life, and thinking, where (as Hebrews tells us) He "had to be made like his brothers in every way, in order that he might become a merciful and faithful high priest in service to God, and that he might make atonement for the sins of the people" (Heb. 2:17).

What He Came to Do

This section begins with the amazing account of Jesus' visit to the synagogue in Nazareth, where the book of Isaiah was brought to Him, and He unrolled it and found the place where it was written:

> *"The Spirit of the Lord is on me, because he has anointed me to preach good news to the poor. He has sent me to proclaim freedom for the prisoners and recovery of sight for the blind, to release the oppressed, to proclaim the year of the Lord's favor" (Luke 4:18–19; see also Isa. 61:1–2).*

Here He declares what He came to do: to enter into the experience of the poor, the oppressed, the blind, the captives, and to set them free. The following chapters then detail His entering into the commonplace human experiences, where people live in darkness, slavery, and death.

At last, in Luke 19:28, we see the Son of Man preparing to enter as the great High Priest into the Holy of Holies of human beings, to restore that which has been lost for all these many centuries. You may remember from your study of the Old Testament that the Holy of Holies contained only two articles of furniture: (1) the ark of the covenant, with its mercy seat under the overarching wings of the cherubim, where God's Shekinah glory dwelt; and (2) the golden altar of incense by means of which the nation was to offer its praise to God. These two objects are symbolic of what is hidden in the depths of humanity.

The mercy seat speaks of human relationship with God. Hebrews tells us that it is blood alone that can make that relationship possible and acceptable:

> *The law requires that nearly everything be cleansed with blood, and without the shedding of blood there is no forgiveness (9:22).*

It was the blood upon the mercy seat that released God's forgiveness and grace. And so our Lord now prepares to enter into the hidden spirit of humanity and offer His own blood. As we are told in Hebrews:

> **It was the blood upon the mercy seat that released God's forgiveness and grace.**

> *He did not enter by means of the blood of goats and calves; but he entered the Most Holy Place once for all by his own blood, having obtained eternal redemption (Heb. 9:12).*

The altar of incense speaks of the communication between people and God—the place of prayer. Prayer is the deepest function of the human spirit. Nothing goes deeper than that. When you are driven to your knees by despair, defeat, exhaustion, or need, you discover that you have reached the rock-bottom resources of your spirit. That is what prayer is at its most fundamental level: the cry of the spirit. So the Cross of Christ enters into this deep, deep region of our humanity.

The Secret Is Revealed

As you continue through Luke, you see the Lord moving from the Mount of Olives down into the city, cleansing the temple, teaching and preaching in the temple, and returning to the mount to deliver the Olivet Discourse. Next, He goes to the Upper Room and the Passover feast, where He institutes the sacrament of Holy Communion. From there He moves on to the Garden of Gethsemane, then to Pilate's judgment seat, and from there to the cross. Then, as we come to the closing chapters, we make a startling and tremendously important discovery:

> *It was now about the sixth hour, and darkness came over the whole land until the ninth hour, for the sun stopped shining. And the curtain of the temple was torn in two (23:44–45).*

Why was this curtain torn in two? Because the Holy of Holies was now to be opened for the first time to human gaze! And because the Holy of Holies of the human spirit was now to be opened for the first time to the gaze and habitation of God!

When the Son of Man died, God ripped the veil wide open. He passed through the holy place, and penetrated into the Holy of Holies, into the secret of humanity—and the reality of humanity's spirit was unveiled.

Resurrection
Morning
Next, we have the wonder of resurrection morning and the account that Luke gives us of the two disciples who were walking on the road to Emmaus when a stranger appeared to them and talked with them. The stranger, of course, was the risen Lord Himself! He opened the Scriptures to these two grieving, uncomprehending disciples—Scriptures concerning Christ and what had been predicted of Him. After Jesus left them, after they realized who He was,

> *They asked each other, "Were not our hearts burning within us while he talked with us on the road and opened the Scriptures to us?" (24.32).*

A burning heart is a heart that is caught up with the excitement and glory of a fulfilled humanity. The secret is revealed. Our humanity is fully possessed, reclaimed by our Creator. The Holy of Holies has been entered. What was lost has been saved.

The perfect parallel to the triumphant message of Luke's Gospel is found in Hebrews 10:19–20:

> *Brothers, since we have confidence to enter the Most Holy Place by the blood of Jesus, by a new and living way opened for us through the curtain, that is, his body . . . .*

That is where we stand now. The secret of humanity is open to anyone who opens his or her heart to the Son of Man, the perfect man. He alone has penetrated the depths of the human spirit. He alone reestablishes the lost relationship with God that enables us to be what God intended us to be. He alone saves and restores what was lost in the fall of man, in the entrance of sin into the world. He alone can restore the marred, distorted image of God in our lives.

All the possibility of a fulfilled humanity is available to anyone in whom the spirit of Christ dwells. All that you deeply want to be in the innermost recesses of your heart, you can be. I'm not talking about your goals in life, such as becoming a millionaire or an Olympic gold medalist. No, I'm talking about the deepest, most inexpressible yearnings of your heart—your desire to be connected to God, to know Him and be known by Him; your desire to have your life count for something in the eternal scheme of things; your desire to be clean and whole and forgiven. Jesus makes it possible for you to fulfill God's best for you, so that you will be mature and Christlike, filled with love, forgiveness, wholeness, and good works.

> Jesus makes it possible for you to fulfill God's best for you.

Why do we act the way we do? Why do we want to do good while doing so much evil? Why are we able to accomplish such great feats of technology, engineering, medical science, athletics, art, literature, and music, yet we cannot eradicate poverty, war, racism, crime, and so many other ills? Where are we heading? What is the aim of it all? The strange mystery of the ages, the great questions that have been raised by philosophers and thinkers about our great but horribly flawed human race—all this has been answered by the entrance of Jesus Christ, the Son of Man, into our humanity.

Luke has unveiled all of this to us in his Gospel, the Gospel of the Son of Man.

NOTES

NOTES

NOTES

NOTES

NOTES

NOTES

ADVENTURING
through the
LIFE *of* CHRIST

CHAPTER FIVE

JOHN:
THE GOD-MAN

J OHN, THE FOURTH GOSPEL, holds a special significance for me for many reasons, but especially because it was written by the disciple closest to our Lord. When you read the Gospel of Matthew, you are reading the record of our Lord as seen through the eyes of a devoted disciple. Mark and Luke, of course, were dedicated followers of Christ who knew and loved Him, though they learned about Him largely through the testimony of others. But John was the beloved apostle who leaned close to Jesus at the Last Supper (13:23–25), who stood at the foot of the cross as the Lord hung dying, and who was trusted by Jesus with the care of His own mother, Mary (19:26–27). John, along with Peter and James, was part of the inner circle of disciples who went with our Lord through the most intimate and dramatic circumstances of His ministry. John heard and saw more than any of the others, which is why John's Gospel is often called "the intimate Gospel."

Who Is This Man?

John's Gospel opens with a startling statement, echoing the opening lines of the book of Genesis:

> *In the beginning was the Word, and the Word was with God, and the Word was God. He was with God in the beginning (John 1:1–2).*

"The Word," of course, is Jesus Christ, and John begins his Gospel with the astonishing statement that Jesus—this man whom John knew so well as a friend and companion—was nothing less than the Creator-God of the universe, who was there at the beginning of all things! John observed the life of Jesus more closely than any other person on earth, and he came away absolutely convinced of the deity of Christ.

Sometimes I think it is difficult to believe that Jesus is God. I've never met a Christian who has not at one time or another felt the full force of all the arguments that make Him out to be nothing more than a human being. There are times when we find it difficult to comprehend the full intent of those words: "In the beginning was the Word."

But if we find it difficult, how much more did His own disciples! They, of all people, would be least likely to believe that He was God, for they lived with Him and saw His humanity as none of us ever has or ever will. They must have been confronted again and again with questions that puzzled and troubled them, such as, "Who is this man? What kind of person is this who heals the sick, raises the dead, quiets the wind, and changes water to wine?" Whatever signs, miracles, power, and wisdom Jesus demonstrated, it must have been a great leap in their perceptions to move from saying of Him, "this man, Jesus," to saying, "My Lord and My God!"

I have often pictured the disciples sleeping out under the stars with our Lord on a summer night by the Sea of Galilee. I can imagine Peter or John or one of the others waking in the night, rising up on an elbow, and as he looked at the Lord Jesus sleeping beside him, saying to himself, "Is it true? Can this man be the eternal God?" No wonder they puzzled over Him and constantly conversed among themselves about the mystery of His actions and His words.

Yet, so overwhelming and convincing was the evidence they saw and heard that when John began to write down the recollections of those amazing days, he began by boldly declaring the deity of Jesus. And that is the theme of the Gospel of John: Jesus is God.

There are actually two endings to the Gospel of John. Chapter 21 reads as a postscript, an add-on, concerning events that occurred after the resurrection. But I believe that John actually ended his Gospel with these words, which are the key to his Gospel:

> *Jesus did many other miraculous signs in the presence of his disciples, which are not recorded in this book. But these are written that you may believe that Jesus is the Christ, the Son of God, and that by believing you may have life in his name (20:30–31).*

Here we see the twofold purpose of this book: (1) John is giving us evidence why anyone in any age, in any place, can fully believe that Jesus is the Christ (or, in the Hebrew form, the Messiah, the Anointed One); and (2) John is showing that Jesus is the Son of God, so that people may have life through belief in His name.

The Outline of John, the Gospel of the Son of God

The Incarnation of the Son of God (John 1:1–18)

1.	His godhood, His forerunner (John the Baptist), His rejection by His own, and His reception by those called "the children of God"	1:1–13
2.	The Word made flesh	1:14–18

The Son of God Is Presented to the World (John 1:19–4:54)

3. Jesus is presented by John the Baptist   1:19–51
4. Jesus begins His ministry in Galilee,   2:1–12
    transforms water into wine at Cana
5. Jesus in Judea, the first cleansing of   2:13–3:36
    the temple and His instruction
    of Nicodemus
6. Jesus in Samaria, the woman at the well   4:1–42
7. Jesus is received in Galilee, heals a   4:43–54
    royal official's son

The Son of God Faces Opposition (John 5:1–12:50)

8. Jesus is opposed at the feast in Jerusalem   5:1–47
9. Jesus is opposed during Passover   6
    in Galilee
10. Jesus is opposed at the Feast of   7–10
    Tabernacles and the Feast of
    Dedication in Jerusalem
11. Jesus is opposed at Bethany; He raises   11
    Lazarus, and the religious leaders plot
    His death
12. Mary anoints Jesus   12:1–11
13. The Triumphal Entry into Jerusalem,   12:12–50
    the opposition of the religious leaders

The Death of the Son of God Approaches (John 13–17)

14. The Upper Room: Jesus washes the   13–14
    disciples' feet and announces His
    approaching death
15. Jesus instructs the disciples in their   15:1–16:15
    relationship to Him, to each other,
    and to the world; He promises the
    Holy Spirit
16. Jesus predicts His death and resurrection   16:16–33
17. Jesus prays in the Garden of   17
    Gethsemane: for Himself, for His
    disciples, for all believers

The Crucifixion and Resurrection of the Son of God (John 18–21)

The Author and the Theme

John did not write his Gospel until the close of the last decade of the first century, and by then he was an old man looking back on all that he had seen, heard, and experienced. John employed the principle of selection as he let his mind run back over the amazing three and a half years he spent with the Lord. This fact has been used by some critics to say that we cannot depend upon the Gospel of John because it is the account of an old man who is trying to recall the events of his youth. Remember, however, that these events were on the heart, tongue, and memory of the apostle John every day of his life. He was always talking about them.

By the time John wrote his Gospel, Matthew, Mark, and Luke had already written theirs, so John ties together and completes the record that they had given of the birth, life, ministry, death, and resurrection of Jesus Christ. Matthew gives us Jesus the King; Mark gives us Jesus the Servant; Luke gives us Jesus the Son of Man; and John gives us Jesus the Son of God.

A great deal is made of the term "Son of God" today, as though there were a distinction to be made between God and the Son of God, but no Hebrew would ever understand it that way. To the Hebrews, to call someone a "son" of something was to say that he was identified with, identical with, that thing or person. For example, the name Barnabas literally means "Son of Consolation." Why? Because he was that kind of man—an encouraging, consoling kind of fellow. His nickname meant that he was the very epitome of consolation—the living, personified expression of encouragement.

To the Hebrews, the use of the term "the Son of God" meant "This man

The Son of God

is God." He was literally the personification of godhood on earth. That is why, invariably, when our Lord used that term when speaking of Himself, He was angrily challenged by the unbelieving scribes and Pharisees. Again and again they demanded of Him, "How dare you! Who do you think you are? You are making yourself out to be equal with God. That's blasphemy!" But it wasn't blasphemy; it was a simple statement of fact.

The Messiah

In John's day, there was a deepening sense of expectation—someone was coming. All through the Old Testament, in book after book, in one way or another, the Scriptures continually repeated the refrain, "Someone is coming! Someone is coming!" Then, at the close of the book of Malachi, there was the throbbing sense of expectation of the "sun of righteousness," the Messiah, who would rise with healing in His wings (Mal. 4:2), and that God would send "the prophet Elijah before that great and dreadful day of the Lord comes" (Mal. 4:5).

People asked themselves, "Is this the one? Is this the Christ, the Messiah promised in the Old Testament?" It was the question on the lips of people in John's day, the question that divided the Jews.

John the Baptist—that fiery, Elijah-like preacher—had appeared. "Are you the Christ?" people asked him. "Are you the one who comes before that great and dreadful day of the Lord?"

"No," said John the Baptist, "but the One you seek is coming after me." And when Jesus began to travel throughout the hills of Judea and Galilee, people wondered, "Is this the one? Is this the Messiah?"

The Lord Jesus declared again and again that He came with the authorized credentials of the Messiah. That is what He meant when He said,

> "I tell you the truth, the man who does not enter the sheep pen by the gate, but climbs in by some other way, is a thief and a robber. The man who enters by the gate is the shepherd of his sheep" (John 10:1–2).

The sheep pen is the nation Israel. Jesus is saying that there is only one (Himself) who comes by an authorized way, by the door. If anyone comes in any other way, he is a thief and a liar, but He who enters by the gate, the authorized opening, will be recognized as the Great Shepherd. He goes on to say,

*"The watchman opens the gate for him, and the sheep listen to his
voice. He calls his own sheep by name and leads them out" (10:3).*

"The watchman" refers to the ministry of John the Baptist, who comes
as the opener of the gate, the forerunner of the Messiah.

As we saw in the Gospel of Luke, Jesus offers His credentials as the one
who is authorized to be the Messiah when He stands in the synagogue at
Nazareth and reads the book of the prophet Isaiah.

*"The Spirit of the Lord is on me, because he has anointed me to
preach good news to the poor. He has sent me to proclaim freedom
for the prisoners and recovery of sight for the blind, to release the
oppressed, to proclaim the year of the Lord's favor" (Luke 4:18–19).*

What does the name *Messiah* mean? "The Anointed One." And what
did Jesus read from the book of Isaiah? "The Spirit of the Lord . . . has
anointed me."

When He stopped reading and put the book aside, He actually stopped
in the middle of a sentence. After the phrase "to proclaim the year of the
Lord's favor," the passage He was reading, Isaiah 61, goes on to say, "and
the day of vengeance of our God." Why didn't He go on and read the rest
of the sentence? Because the day of vengeance had not yet come. Jesus, in
His first coming, came to fulfill the first half of the messianic mission—to
preach good news to the poor, to heal the brokenhearted, to set the captives free. The second half of the messianic mission—to proclaim the day
of God's vengeance—would await His second coming.

So, after Jesus stopped reading at that point in Isaiah 61, He closed the
book, sat down, and said to everyone gathered in the synagogue, "Today
this scripture is fulfilled in your hearing" (Luke 4:21). In other words,
"This Scripture passage is about Me. I am the promised Messiah."

The Marks of the Messiah

To demonstrate the authority of Jesus as God's Anointed One, the
Messiah, John selects seven events from the ministry of Jesus—seven marks
of the Messiah. Let's examine them in the order in which they appear in
John's Gospel:

First mark of the Messiah: the first miracle of our Lord—the changing
of water into wine (John 2:1–11). This miracle was actually a visible parable. Our Lord performed a profoundly symbolic act at the wedding in

> **God's purpose is to take human beings in their brokenness, their emptiness, and their lifelessness and to give them life.**

Cana of Galilee. He took something that belonged to the realm of the inanimate world—water—and changed it into a living substance, wine. He took something that belonged to the realm of mere matter and changed it into something that is forever an expression of joy and life. By this act, He declared in symbol what He came to do: to proclaim the acceptable year of the Lord. He came to declare the day of grace, when God's purpose is to take human beings in their brokenness, their emptiness, and their lifelessness and to give them life.

Second mark of the Messiah: the healing of the royal official's son (John 4:46–54). The central figure in this story is not the son, who lies sick and dying, but the official, who comes to the Lord with a grief-broken heart. In his agony, the official cries out to Jesus, the Christ, and says, "Will you come down and heal my son?" The Lord not only heals the son at a distance with just a word (the same creative power that brought the world into being), but He heals the broken heart of the father. As Jesus said, He was anointed to heal the brokenhearted.

Third mark of the Messiah: the healing of the paralyzed man who lay at the pool of Bethesda (John 5:1–9). Remember, that man had lain there for thirty-eight years. He had been a prisoner of this paralyzing disease, so that he was unable to get into the pool. He had been brought to the pool in the hope that he might be healed, hoping to be set free—and the Lord singled him out of the great crowd and healed him, saying to him, "Get up! Pick up your mat and walk." Here Jesus demonstrated His ability to set at liberty those who are oppressed and imprisoned. For thirty-eight years a man had been bound, yet Jesus instantly set him free.

Fourth mark of the Messiah: the feeding of the five thousand (John 6:1–14). This miracle appears in all four of the Gospels. Linked with it is the miracle of Jesus walking on the water. What is the meaning of these signs? You cannot read the story of the feeding of the five thousand without seeing that it is a marvelous demonstration of the Lord's desire to meet the deepest need of the human heart, the hunger for God. He uses the symbol of bread, having Himself said, "It is written: 'Man does not live on bread alone, but on every word that comes from the mouth of God'" (Matthew 4:4). Then He demonstrates what kind of bread He means, saying, "I am the bread of life" (John 6:35). Taking the bread, He broke it, and with it fed the five thousand, symbolizing how fully He can meet the need and hunger of human souls.

Fifth mark of the Messiah: walking on water. After the feeding of the five thousand, Jesus sends His disciples out into the storm—then He comes walking across the waves to them in the midst of the tempest. The waves are high, the ship is about to be overwhelmed, and their hearts are clenched with fear. Jesus comes to them, quiets their fears, and says, "It is I; don't be afraid" (John 6:20). The double miracle of the feeding of the five thousand and the walking on water provides a symbolic representation of our Lord's ability to satisfy the need of human hearts and deliver people from their greatest enemy, fear. This is good news! And this is one of the signs of the Messiah: He came to proclaim good news to the poor.

Sixth mark of the Messiah: the healing of the blind man (John 9:1–12). This story hardly needs comment. Our Lord said that He came "to give recovery of sight to the blind" (Luke 4:18). He chose a man who was blind from birth, just as human beings are spiritually blind from birth, and He healed him.

Seventh mark of the Messiah: the raising of Lazarus from the dead (John 11:1–44). This symbolizes the deliverance of those who all their lives had been held under the bondage of the fear of death.

These seven signs prove beyond question that Jesus is the Messiah. He is the Anointed One, promised by God in the Old Testament.

John's theme is twofold: First, when you see Jesus in His delivering power, you are indeed seeing the promised Deliverer, the Messiah. But that is not the greatest secret to be revealed about Him. Throughout the centuries of Old Testament history, an astounding secret had been guarded. Prophets down through the ages had expected the coming of the Messiah, a great man of God. But who could have known, who could have imagined, who could have expected that this great man of God would be, in fact, the Son of God, the very person of God in human form? For that is John's second theme: Jesus is God.

When you stand in the presence of the Lord's humanity, you can see His loving eyes, feel the beating of His human heart, sense the compassion of His life poured out in service to other human beings. Yet the amazing truth is that when you stand in His presence, you stand in the presence of God Himself! You see what God Himself is like! In the opening chapter of his Gospel, John makes this statement:

> These seven signs prove beyond question that Jesus is the Messiah.

> *No one has ever seen God, but [the Son] the One and Only, who is at the Father's side, has made him known (1:18).*

"No one has ever seen God." That is a statement of fact. People hunger for God, and they are always searching for God, but no one has ever seen Him. But John goes on to say that the Son has made Him known. Jesus has unfolded what God is like. [Note: Some Greek manuscripts of John 1:18 use the word *God* in the place where I have bracketed the words "the Son." The NIV text followed those manuscripts, using the word *God* in that place. But I believe the clearer and more accurate translation is the one I have indicated, "the Son."]

The Seven "I Ams"

In his Gospel, John records seven great words of our Lord that prove his claim that Jesus is the Son of God. He bases it all on the great name of God revealed to Moses at the burning bush. When Moses saw the bush burning and turned aside to learn its secret, God spoke to him from the bush and said, "I AM WHO I AM" (Ex. 3:14). That is God's expression of His own self-consistent, self-perpetuating, self-existent nature. He says, "I am exactly what I am—no more, no less. I am the eternal I am." Seven times in John's Gospel he picks up this expression as it was used by Jesus Himself. These "I am" statements of Jesus constitute the proof that He is God.

> These "I am" statements of Jesus constitute the proof that He is God.

You may have thought that Jesus' miracles establish His claim of deity. But no, they only establish the fact that He is the Messiah, the Promised One. His words establish His claim to be God. Listen to those words from His own lips:

"I am the bread of life" (6:35). In other words, "I am the sustainer of life, the One who satisfies life."

"I am the light of the world" (8:12). Jesus is telling us He is the illuminator of life, the explainer of all things, the one who casts light upon all mysteries and enigmas of life—and solves them.

"I am the gate" (10:7). Jesus states that He is the only opening that leads to eternal life. He is the open way.

"I am the good shepherd" (10:11). Jesus is the guide of life, the only one who is able to safely steer us and protect us through all the perils and chasms that yawn on every side. He is the one whose rod of discipline and staff of guidance can comfort us, give us peace, lead us beside still waters, and restore our souls.

"I am the resurrection and the life" (11:25). He is the miraculous power of life, the giver and restorer of life. Resurrection power is the only power that saves when all hope is lost. Resurrection power works in the midst of despair, failure, and even death. When nothing else can be done, Jesus appears and says, "I am the resurrection and the life."

"I am the way and the truth and the life" (14:6). That is, "I am ultimate reality. I am the real substance behind all things."

"I am the vine. . . . apart from me you can do nothing" (15:5). I am the producer of all fruitfulness, the reason of all fellowship, the source of all identity and communion.

Seven times our Lord makes an "I am" statement, taking the great, revealing name of God from the Old Testament and linking it with simple yet profound symbols for the New Testament, using picture after picture to enable us to understand God.

The Message that Requires a Response

John 1:14 announces, "The Word became flesh and made his dwelling among us. We have seen his glory, the glory of the One and Only, who came from the Father, full of grace and truth." The phrase "and made his dwelling among us" literally means that He tabernacled among us, or, He pitched His tent among us. All the glory that is God became a human being. That is the tremendous theme of this book. There is no greater theme in all the universe than the fact that we stand in the presence of both the full humanity and the full deity of Jesus. He is the God-man. He shows us what God is like. He is the One who heals, loves, serves, waits, blesses, dies, and rises again—this is the ultimate human being, and this is God. That is the truth revealed in the Gospel of John.

Near the end of his Gospel, John writes, "These are written that you may believe that Jesus is the Christ, the Son of God, and that by believing you may have life in his name" (20:31). Jesus is the key to life. We all want to live—old and young alike. We all seek the key to life. We seek fulfillment. These are our deepest yearnings. And when we come to the end of our search, we find Jesus waiting for us with open arms. He is the goal of all our searching, all our desiring. He makes us to be all we were designed to be.

The Gospel of John does not simply present us with a story about Jesus. It does not simply inform us or even inspire us. It confronts us. It makes a demand on us. It requires a response. By forcing us to recognize the authentic deity of

> John calls us to either worship Jesus or to reject Him.

Christ, John calls us to either worship Him or reject Him. There is no middle ground.

How can you stand in the presence of this divine mystery, in the shadow of the God-man who made the universe, then died upon a lonely hill, and not feel your heart drawn to worship Him? As we often sing,

> And can it be that I should gain
> An interest in my Savior's blood?
> Died He for me, who caused His pain?
> For me, who Him to death pursued?
> Amazing love, how can it be
> That thou, my God, shouldst die for me?
> —*Charles Wesley*

True Worship

That is true worship—a recognition that Jesus is God, and that God has submitted Himself to death on our behalf! And true worship leads us to action, to service, to obedience. As in the words of the hymn, "Love so amazing, so divine, demands my soul, my life, my all."

When our hearts are filled with true worship, when our hands are engaged in true service, we are united with the One who made the entire universe, the One who is the great "I am." That is a thrilling, exalting thought.

And that is the message of the Gospel of John.

NOTES

NOTES

NOTES

NOTES

NOTES

ADVENTURING
through the
LIFE *of* CHRIST

CHAPTER SIX

ACTS:
THE UNFINISHED
STORY

WHEN I WAS A STUDENT at Dallas Theological Seminary, each of us seminarians had to take a turn at preaching while the other students listened and evaluated. By watching and listening to these preachers-in-training, I could tell what great preacher had influenced each of them. Some of the young men had come from Bob Jones University, and they would stand on one leg, lean over the pulpit, shout and wave their arms just like Bob Jones. Others clearly came from a Young Life background—they would stand with their hands in their pockets, gesture with a closed fist, and drawl just like Young Life's Jim Rayburn. In seminarian after seminarian, I recognized various influences.

I also noticed something else: While these seminary students imitated the virtues of their pulpit heroes, they also tended to imitate their faults. That, I think, is what many Christians and many churches have done with the book of Acts. We have studied the example of the early church, as recorded in Acts, and we have imitated that church—faults and all! So as we examine the record of the early church, we should avoid any superficial analysis. Even though our survey of Acts in this handbook will be relatively brief and concise, we will try to make sure it is not superficial.

Acts is the book that reveals the power of the church. Whenever a church in our own century begins to lose its power, to turn dull and drab in its witness, it needs to rediscover the book of Acts. It is the story of the Holy Spirit's entering into a small group of believers, filling them with power and enthusiasm from on high, and *exploding* them—sending them like a shower of flaming embers into the world, igniting new fires and starting new churches. That is how the gospel spread like wildfire in the first century A.D.

> **Acts is the book that reveals the power of the church.**

The Book of the Revolving Door

I like to think of the book of Acts as a revolving door. A revolving door is designed to allow people to go in and out at the same time: They go in one side and go out the other. The book of Acts is like that—Old Testament Judaism is going out and the New Testament church is coming in. Both are in the revolving door at the same time for a while, just as two people can be in a revolving door going in opposite directions. But don't ever try to set up housekeeping in a revolving door—you'll get knocked off your feet! A revolving door is not designed for habitation; it is designed for transition, for movement.

In a similar way, we should not rely exclusively on the book of Acts for doctrine and teaching. It is not designed for that. It is a book of history, of fast-moving events, of transition. Acts is designed to stir us up, to encourage us and bless us, and to show us what God intends to do through the church, but it is not primarily a book of doctrine.

> **Acts is a book of history, of fast-moving events, of transition—not doctrine.**

The book of Acts was written by Luke, Paul's beloved companion, the author of the Gospel of Luke. Unfortunately, it bears the wrong title. In most editions and translations of Scripture it is called The Acts of the Apostles. But as you read the book through, the only apostles whose acts are highlighted are Peter and Paul. Most other apostles go largely unnoticed in Acts. The book should really be titled The Acts of the Holy Spirit— or even more appropriately, The Continuing Acts of the Lord Jesus Christ. You can actually find this suggestion in the introduction of the book. As Luke writes to the same friend he addressed in his Gospel, he says,

> *In my former book, Theophilus, I wrote about all that Jesus began to do and to teach . . . (Acts 1:1).*

Obviously, then, Luke was volume 1 and Acts is volume 2. Acts is the sequel, the continuation of what Jesus began both to do and to teach. Luke goes on to say,

> *. . . until the day he was taken up to heaven, after giving instructions through the Holy Spirit to the apostles he had chosen. After his suffering, he showed himself to these men and gave many convincing proofs that he was alive. He appeared to them over a period of forty days and spoke about the kingdom of God. On one occasion, while he was eating with them, he gave them this command: "Do not leave Jerusalem, but wait for the gift my Father promised, which you have heard me speak about. For John baptized with water, but in a few days you will be baptized with the Holy Spirit" (1:2–5).*

This is the essence of the book of Acts. It is the account of the way the Holy Spirit, moving through the church, continued what Jesus began to do in His earthly ministry.

The record of the Gospels is *only the beginning* of the story of the work of the Lord Jesus Christ. When you come to the end of the Gospels, you have come not to the end, nor even to the beginning of the end, but to the end of the beginning. In the book of Acts, the Holy Spirit begins to fulfill the program of God by carrying on His work through the church.

> We now live in the age of the Spirit—an age inaugurated on the day of Pentecost, the first major event of the book of Acts.

When Jesus ascended into heaven, He exchanged His own resurrected body on earth for a different kind of body on earth—the church, which the New Testament calls "the body of Christ." Instead of a single human body that can be in either Galilee or Samaria or Judea and that must stop every now and then to sleep, He now has a body that reaches to the uttermost parts of the earth and is active twenty-four hours a day!

We now live in the age of the Spirit—an age inaugurated on the day of Pentecost, the first major event of the book of Acts.

The Outline of the Book of Acts

We can find the outline of the book of Acts in a well-known verse (Acts 1:8)—our Lord's final words to His disciples just before He was taken up into heaven:

> *"You will receive power when the Holy Spirit comes on you; and you will be my witnesses in Jerusalem, and in all Judea and Samaria, and to the ends of the earth."*

"You will receive power when the Holy Spirit comes on you" encompasses the first two chapters of Acts—the chapters concerning the coming of the Holy Spirit. "And you will be my witnesses" establishes the theme of the rest of Acts, chapters 3 through 28. The concluding phrase, "in Jerusalem, and in all Judea and Samaria, and to the ends of the earth," then divides chapters 3 through 28 into several parts:

As we study the book of Acts, we will see how this outline of the book, which was inspired by the Holy Spirit, is literally fulfilled by the Holy Spirit in the life of the early church. The story of Acts begins in Jerusalem, the center of the Jewish nation, and it ends in Rome, the center of the Gentile world. It carries us from the limited gospel of the kingdom at the close of the four Gospels through the spreading of the gospel of grace to the whole world at the close of Acts. With this structure as our foundation, here is an overview of the book of Acts:

The Coming of the Holy Spirit (Acts 1–2)

1. Prologue: the resurrection, appearance,   1:1–10
   and ascension of Jesus Christ
2. The promise of the Holy Spirit   1:11
3. The appointment of replacement   1:12–26
   apostle Matthias
4. Pentecost, the dramatic entrance of   2
   the Spirit

The Witness of the Holy Spirit from Jerusalem to the Ends of the Earth (Acts 3–28)

5. The witness of the Holy Spirit   3–7
   in Jerusalem
   A. Peter heals and preaches   3
   B. Peter and John minister in chains   4:1–31
   C. Early church grows and shares   4:32–37
   D. Ananias and Sapphira: don't lie   5:1–11
      to the Holy Spirit
   E. Miracles of the apostles   5:12–16
   F. Persecution of the apostles   5:17–42
   G. Deacons appointed, Stephen   6–7
      martyred
6. The witness of the Holy Spirit in all   8–12
   Judea and Samaria
   A. Saul persecutes the church   8:1–3
   B. The witness of Philip to the Samar-   8:4–40
      itans and the Ethiopian eunuch
   C. The conversion of Saul (Paul)   9:1–31
   D. The witness of Peter, including   9:32–11:18
      healings, raising Dorcas, witness-
      ing to Cornelius, beginning
      of the ministry to the Gentiles
   E. The witness of the Antioch church   11:19–30
   F. Herod persecutes the church   12
7. The witness of the Holy Spirit to the   13–28
   ends of the earth
   A. The first missionary journey of   13–14
      Saul/Paul and Barnabas

B. The Jerusalem Council,   15:1–35
law vs. grace

C. The second missionary journey,   15:36–18:22
including the argument between
Paul and Barnabas over John
Mark, 15:36–41; the ministry at
Philippi and the conversion of
the Philippian jailer, 16; the
Bereans search the Scriptures,
17:10–15; Paul's ministry with
Aquila and Priscilla, 18:1–3

D. The third missionary journey   18:23–21:16

E. Paul turns toward Rome   21:17–28:31

The Restoration of the Twelve

Following the death of Judas Iscariot, the disciple who betrayed Jesus, Peter stands and says to the church, "For it is written in the book of Psalms, 'May his place be deserted; let there be no one to dwell in it,' and, 'May another take his place of leadership' " (1:20). Thus, one of the first actions the believers in Jerusalem take after the ascension of Christ is to determine whom God wants to step into the empty place of leadership left by Judas. The lot falls to Matthias, and the number of the apostles is restored to twelve.

Why was this necessary? Because there had to be twelve apostles to faithfully carry out the apostolic ministry, and it was upon The Twelve that the Holy Spirit was poured out on the day of Pentecost. (It is important and interesting to note that in the book of Revelation the names of the twelve apostles form the foundations of the city that John saw coming down from heaven—the restored twelve, that is. See Rev. 21:14.)

However, it also appears that the office of Judas was actually filled by not one man but two. While Matthias became the replacement apostle to Israel, the apostle Paul became the special apostle to the Gentiles. This does not mean that the other apostles did not have a ministry to the Gentiles, for they certainly did. In fact, it was to Peter that God gave a vision showing him that the Gospel was to go out to the Gentiles as well as to the house of Israel (see Acts 10). But while God chose Peter to be the chief apostle to Israel, Paul went primarily to the Gentiles. The other apostles were divinely chosen as a witness to Israel, and they fulfilled that ministry completely.

The Outpouring of the Holy Spirit

After the full number of apostles was restored, the great mark of the book of Acts—the pouring out of the Holy Spirit—took place. Everything else flows from this event in Acts 2. The interesting thing is to see how Christians, reading about this amazing occurrence, have focused their attention on the incidentals and neglected the essentials.

The incidentals here—the rushing wind, the fire that danced on the heads of the disciples, and the many tongues or languages by which they spoke—are simply the peripheral events that took place, the signs that showed that something important was happening.

The essential event was the formation of a new and distinct community, the church. One hundred and twenty individuals met in the temple courts. They were as unrelated to each other as any people born in widely scattered parts of the earth can be. But when the Holy Spirit was poured out on them, He baptized them into one body. They became a living unit. They were no longer related only to the Lord; they also were related to each other as brothers and sisters in Christ. They were the body of Christ.

As the body of Christ, they received a new program, a new purpose. With the Holy Spirit dwelling in them, they began to reach out to Jerusalem and then beyond, to Judea, Samaria, and the uttermost parts of the earth.

The same body of Christ that came into existence at Pentecost is alive today and will remain alive, active, and energized until the day of the Lord's return. That is the essential and important fact of Acts 2: The birth of the body, the beginning of the church. It is this body that the Holy Spirit inhabits and into which He breathes His power and life. Through this body, the Spirit of God is active in the world today, carrying out His eternal plan.

> **The same body of Christ that came into existence at Pentecost is alive today.**

The Calling of Paul

The rest of the book of Acts deals largely with the calling and ministry of the apostle Paul—the wise master builder, the one whom the Holy Spirit selected to be the pattern for Gentile Christians. This is why Paul was put through such an intensive training period by the Holy Spirit, during which he was subjected to one of the most rigorous trials that any human being could undergo. He was sent back to his own hometown to live in obscurity for seven years, until he had learned the great lesson that the Holy Spirit seeks to teach every Christian—the lesson without which no one can ever be effective for Him. In the words of our Lord, "I tell you the truth, unless a kernel of wheat falls to the ground and dies, it remains only a single seed. But if it dies, it produces many seeds" (John 12:24).

As you trace the career of the apostle Paul, you discover that (like most of us) he didn't understand this principle when he first came to Christ. He thought that he had all it took. He believed that he was especially prepared to be the kind of instrument that could be mightily used by God to win Israel to Christ. Undoubtedly (as he reveals in Phil. 3:4–6; compare Acts 22:3), he had the background; he had the training. He was by birth a Hebrew; he was educated in all the law and the understanding of the Hebrews; he had the position; he was the favorite pupil of the greatest teacher of Israel, Gamaliel; he was a Pharisee of the Pharisees; he understood everything of the Hebrew law, faith, and culture.

Again and again in his letters, you see Paul's hungering to be an instrument to reach Israel for Christ. In Romans, he writes, "I have great sorrow and unceasing anguish in my heart. For I could wish that I myself were cursed and cut off from Christ for the sake of my brothers, those of my own race" (Rom. 9:2–3). But God had said to this man, "I don't want you to go to Israel with the Gospel. I'm calling you to be the apostle to the Gentiles, to bear My name before kings and to preach to the Gentiles the unsearchable riches of Christ."

After Paul tried in Damascus to preach Christ out of the energy of his own flesh and found that he was failing, he was driven out of the city and let down like a criminal over the wall in a basket. Brokenhearted and defeated, he found his way to Jerusalem and thought the apostles at least would take him in, but they turned him aside. It was only when Barnabas finally interceded for him that he was given any acceptance in the eyes of the apostles.

> **Unless Paul was willing to die to his own ambition to be the apostle to Israel, he could never be the servant of Christ.**

Then, going into the temple, Paul met the Lord, who said to him, "Go back home. Get out of the city. They won't receive your testimony here. This isn't the place I've called you to" (see Acts 22:17–21). Back home in Tarsus, he at last faced up to what God was saying to him: Unless he was willing to die to his own ambition to be the apostle to Israel, he could never be the servant of Christ. And when at last he received that commission and took it to heart, he said, "Lord, anywhere you want. Anything you want. Anywhere you want to send me. I'm ready to go." God sent

Barnabas to him, and he took him by the hand and led him down to Antioch, a Gentile church, and there the apostle Paul began his ministry.

The Advance of the Gospel

The book of Acts ends with Paul in Rome, preaching in his own hired house, chained day and night to a Roman guard, unable to go out as a missionary. He is a prisoner; yet his heart overflows with the consciousness that though he is bound, the Word of God is not. Thus, as he writes to his friends in Philippi, he says, "Now I want you to know, brothers, that what has happened to me has really served to advance the gospel" (Phil. 1:12). These obstacles and disappointments have not stopped a thing; they have only advanced the gospel.

Paul cites two specific ways in which the gospel was being advanced:

1. The praetorian guard was being reached for Christ (Phil. 1:12–13).

At the emperor's command, the Roman guards were chained to the apostle for six hours at a time. Talk about a captive audience! God was using the emperor to expose his best men to hours of instruction in the Christian gospel! And one by one, these Roman soldiers who were guarding Paul were coming to know Christ. No wonder Paul writes at the end of the letter, "All the saints send you greetings, especially those who belong to Caesar's household" (Phil. 4:22).

2. Because of Paul's arrest, the other believers in the city were preaching the gospel with increased power and boldness (Phil. 1:14).

"Because of my chains," Paul wrote, "most of the brothers in the Lord have been encouraged to speak the word of God more courageously and fearlessly." Ironically, the gospel was going out across Rome with even greater force and intensity since Paul had been in prison because people had stopped relying on Paul as the sole evangelist to Rome. If the job of evangelizing Rome was going to happen, other people were going to have to pick up where Paul left off and carry on in his place. And Paul said, "I rejoice in that." (I have often wondered if the best way to evangelize a city might be to lock up all the preachers in jail!)

There was another advantage to Paul's imprisonment in Rome—an advantage that even the apostle himself could not have imagined. We can see now, with the perspective of two thousand years of hindsight, that the greatest work Paul did in his lifetime was not to go about preaching

Obstacles and Disappointments Advance the Gospel

> Paul's greatest accomplishment was the body of letters he wrote—many of which were written from prison.

the gospel and planting churches, as great as that work was. *His greatest accomplishment was the body of letters he wrote, many of which were written in prison*—many of which perhaps would never have been written if he had not been in prison. Because of those letters, the church has been nurtured, strengthened, and emboldened through twenty centuries of Christian history.

The Error of the Church

For many centuries the church has suffered from a tragic misconception. In fact, much of the weakness of the church today is due to this misconception that has developed within the body of Christ. For centuries, Christians have met together and recited the Great Commission of Jesus Christ to take the gospel out to the farthest corners of the earth: "Therefore go and make disciples of all nations, baptizing them in the name of the Father and of the Son and of the Holy Spirit" (Matt. 28:19). And that is unquestionably the will of God. But it is one of the favorite tricks of the devil to get Christians to pursue God's will in their own way, according to their own limited wisdom, in pursuit of their own will.

It is never possible to truly fulfill God's will in a human way. Yet that is exactly what the church has been doing. We have gathered ourselves together, recited the Great Commission, and said, "Now we must mobilize all our human resources to plan the strategy for carrying out God's will." Christ is often pictured as waiting in heaven, earnestly hoping that we will get with it down here and carry out His program. According to this view, His plan for the world hinges on our strategies, our ingenuity, our effort. Without our human strength, Jesus would never get the job done. This view is a satanic deception.

Why have we become deceived? Because we have listened to only part of the Great Commission.

> *"Therefore go and make disciples of all nations, baptizing them*
> *in the name of the Father and of the Son and of the Holy Spirit,*
> *and teaching them to obey everything I have commanded you.*
> *And surely I am with you always, to the very end of the age"*
> *(Matt. 28:19–20).*

We have heard and carried out the first part—the "going." We have strategized and mobilized and gone "to the ends of the earth." But we have almost completely forgotten the last part of that commission: "And surely

I am with you always, to the very end of the age."

The Lord never intended that we should try to fulfill the Great Commission in our own strength, while He stands by and watches. He is with us always— and we must allow Him to be in charge of His own strategy for reaching the world.

> The Lord never intended that we should try to fulfill the Great Commission in our own strength, while He stands by and watches.

When we come back to Him exhausted, beaten, and discouraged—as we inevitably are—and we cry out to Him, "Oh, Lord, we can never get this job done. We can never accomplish this," He will remind us that His program is for the Holy Spirit to accomplish this task through the church. That, after all, is what the book of Acts is about: how the Holy Spirit carried out His program and exploded ministry throughout the known world. God did not call the apostles and the early church to do all the work. Instead, the message of Acts is the same message that Paul gives us in 1 Thessalonians 5:24: "The one who calls you is faithful and he will do it." It was always God's intention not only to lay the program before us, but to fulfill it in His own strength.

The Divine Strategy

As you read through the book of Acts, you see various aspects of the ministry of the Holy Spirit. First of all, He is visible in directing the activities of the church. It is the Spirit of God—not human beings—who takes the initiative and launches new movements in carrying out the program of God. For example, when Philip was in Samaria preaching the gospel, a great citywide revival was in progress as a result of his preaching. The whole city was swept with the spirit of revival.

Human wisdom would say, "Hey, we've got something going here! Let's invest more resources in Samaria! Let's really expand our evangelistic mission in Samaria! Let's develop a big 'Win Samaria for Jesus' strategy!" But that wasn't God's plan. Instead, as in Acts 8, the Spirit of God tells Philip to go to the desert and find a man—a lone Ethiopian man—and witness to him.

Now, what kind of strategy is that, to leave a citywide campaign where the Spirit of God is moving in power, where multitudes are coming to Christ, only to go down into the desert to talk to one man? And who was this man?

He was the treasurer of the Ethiopian government, and the Holy Spirit had already been preparing his heart for his encounter with Philip.

As Philip came alongside the chariot of the Ethiopian, he saw that the man was reading from Isaiah 53—a powerful Old Testament prophecy of the Messiah. Philip asked the man if he understood what he read, and the man answered with a rhetorical question: "How can I, unless someone explains it to me?" So Philip sat beside him and told him the story of the Messiah who had finally come, who had suffered and died, and who had been raised again. And Philip won the man to Christ on the spot.

The influential Ethiopian official returned to his own country, and tradition holds that many Ethiopians were led to Christ through him, and through him the reach of the gospel was first extended to the continent of Africa.

> Spirit-led witnessing is about the right person in the right place at the right time saying the right thing to the right person.

That is always what Spirit-led witnessing is about: The right person in the right place at the right time saying the right thing to the right person. This is one of the first evidences in the book of Acts of the overall directing activity of the Holy Spirit.

In Acts 9, the Holy Spirit reaches a man on the Damascus road and sends another man to pray with him—Ananias, who is absolutely astounded by this commission. "Lord," Ananias prays, "you don't know what you are asking! This man is the chief persecutor of Your church!" God replies, "I know whom I have called. He's a chosen instrument of Mine." And the man whom God sent Ananias to was—of course!—Saul, the future apostle Paul.

In chapter 13, the church at Antioch fasts and prays, and in the midst of their worship the Holy Spirit tells the church, "Set apart for me Barnabas and Saul for the work to which I have called them" (13:2). Later, we read,

> *Paul and his companions traveled throughout the region of Phrygia and Galatia, having been kept by the Holy Spirit from preaching the word in the province of Asia. When they came to the border of Mysia, they tried to enter Bithynia, but the Spirit of Jesus would not allow them to (16:6–7).*

All through Acts you find that the divine strategy has all been worked out in advance—not by people but by the Holy Spirit. As Christians are available to the Spirit, He unfolds the strategy step by step. Nobody can plan this kind of a program. We can only be willing to follow the overall directive activity of the Spirit of God at work in His church. That is the divine strategy.

And how do we discover and lay hold of the divine strategy? By following the example of a "noble" group of people we find in Acts 17:

> *As soon as it was night, the brothers sent Paul and Silas away to Berea. On arriving there, they went to the Jewish synagogue. Now the Bereans were of more noble character than the Thessalonians, for they received the message with great eagerness and examined the Scriptures every day to see if what Paul said was true. Many of the Jews believed, as did also a number of prominent Greek women and many Greek men (17:10–12).*

If only we were more like the noble Bereans, who eagerly examined the Scriptures, comparing Paul's words with the Word of God! If only we would search the Scriptures for ourselves instead of allowing ourselves to be spoon-fed by this pastor or that Christian author.

The Example of the Noble Bereans

Even as you and I are adventuring through the Gospel and Acts together in this book, I hope that you will never simply take my word on any matter of spiritual truth. Rather, I encourage you to be like the noble Bereans. Check God's Word for yourself, listen to the Holy Spirit's leading, pray to God—and when you pray, listen quietly for His answer. Seek the mind of God and the understanding that comes from His Word and His Spirit. That is the noble thing to do!

Instruments of the Spirit

Later in Acts we find the Holy Spirit engaged in another aspect of His ministry, doing what no human being can do: communicating life to those who hear the gospel. Wherever the message of salvation is preached, wherever the Word of God is upheld, the Holy Spirit is there to communicate life.

Have you ever noticed who gives the altar call in the book of Acts? It is almost invariably the ones being preached to, not the preachers! On the day of Pentecost, as the Spirit of God preached through Peter to the thousands attracted by the Holy Spirit's amazing miracle of the tongues of flame and the tongues of languages, Peter's audience was so convicted by the Spirit that they interrupted him in mid-sermon! "What must we do to be saved?" they shouted (paraphrase; see Acts 2:37). Peter didn't have to give the altar call—his audience beat him to it!

And in Acts 16, when the Philippian jailer was impressed by the singing of Paul and Silas at midnight, and then the earthquake shook the prison walls to the ground, who gave the altar call? The Philippian jailer himself! He came running and asked them, "Sirs, what must I do to be saved?"

In case after case, incident after incident, it was the Holy Spirit, communicating to needy hearts, preparing them in advance to believe and respond when the message came to them.

Maintaining Doctrinal Purity Is the Work of the Holy Spirit

Today there are many Christian groups and individuals whose sole occupation in life seems to be to defend the faith—to preserve, if they can, the purity of the church. Many of these people go so far as to corner unsuspecting pastors, inspect every sentence and clause of their sermons for hints or suggestions of unorthodox belief or faulty doctrine, then nail them to the wall for even the most minor or dubious whiff of "heresy." While it is proper to want the church to be pure and true to the Scriptures, the book of Acts shows us that it is the Spirit of God Himself who is in charge of this task.

As the church fulfills its commission to be available, to be willing instruments of the activity and life of the Holy Spirit, He is at work to preserve the purity of the church. For example, there is an amazing incident recorded early in the book of Acts: Ananias and Sapphira's hypocrisy. Their sin was revealed when they tried to attach to themselves a holiness that they did not actually possess (Acts 5:1–11). They tried to appear more committed or dedicated than they really were. They tried to gain a reputation for sanctity among their fellow Christians by appearance only. And the judgment of the Holy Spirit came immediately in the form of their physical death.

I do not believe that God exercises such dramatic judgment in the church today. Rather, through His Word, God presents Ananias and Sapphira as an example for us, a pattern to indicate what the Spirit of God does on the spiritual level. In the early church He judged these two hypocrites on the physical level in order that we might see this principle at work. But whether spiritual or physical, the result is exactly the same.

Let somebody begin to use his religious standing, her Christian opportunities, to elevate his own proud reputation in the eyes of people, to pretend to a holiness she does not possess, and what happens? The Spirit of God cuts them off from the manifestation of the life of Christ! Instantly that individual's life is as powerless, as weak and fruitless, as dead and lacking in effect, as the dead bodies of Ananias and Sapphira lying at the feet of Peter. It is a sobering principle of the Christian life, and one that every believer should consider seriously and honestly, while examining his or her own life.

Christians were the wonder and sensation of the first-century world. The message they preached and the way they lived had the entire known world in a commotion. What was it about these people that set the entire world abuzz? Only one thing: The Spirit of God was alive in them! The Spirit gave them power, energy, excitement, courage, and boldness—especially boldness!

> Christians were the wonder and sensation of the first-century world.

Notice their boldness: One moment, near the end of the Gospels, you see Peter and John hiding behind locked doors, afraid to go out into the streets of Jerusalem for fear of those who hated and crucified the Lord Jesus. But now, after the Spirit of God comes upon them, they are out in the streets and temple courts boldly proclaiming the truth of Jesus Christ. When they are locked up in prison, the angel releases them and they go right back into the temple courts to pray and preach again. They are unstoppable! They are invincible! And every time they are arrested or rioted against or stoned or beaten, what do these Christians pray for? Not safety. Not protection. No, they pray for even more boldness!

That is God's program. The Holy Spirit does everything in the book of Acts. He does all the energizing, guiding, directing, programming, empowering, preparing, and communicating. He does it all. It is not up to us to do anything except to be available, to be His instruments, to go where He wills, to open our mouths and speak His words, to be ready to take advantage of whatever situation He places us in. It is the job of the Spirit to carry out that ministry. That is why this book should be called the Acts of the Holy Spirit of God not the Acts of the Apostles.

That is what the church lacks today. We want to do all the right things, but we try to do them in our own strength, according to our own wisdom, employing our own strategy, writing the Book of Our Own Acts for God rather than continuing the story of the Acts of the Holy Spirit of God. That is a tragedy that breaks the heart of God, and it should break our hearts as well.

The Unfinished Book

The book of Acts concludes abruptly, with these words:

For two whole years Paul stayed there in his own rented house and welcomed all who came to see him. Boldly and without hindrance he preached the kingdom of God and taught about the Lord Jesus Christ (28:30–31).

We know, of course, that this is not the end of Paul's story. In Acts 20:24 and 38, Paul talks about his approaching death. In 2 Timothy 4:6–8, he writes with an obvious sense that his days are numbered:

I am already being poured out like a drink offering, and the time has come for my departure. I have fought the good fight, I have finished the race, I have kept the faith. Now there is in store for me the crown of righteousness, which the Lord, the righteous Judge, will award to me on that day—and not only to me, but also to all who have longed for his appearing.

According to tradition, Paul was executed in Rome in February, A.D. 62. The fact that Acts does not record Paul's death, nor does it refer to such important events as the persecution under Nero (A.D. 64) or the destruction of Jerusalem (A.D. 70), suggests that the book of Acts was probably written before Paul's death. In any case, the book of Acts is clearly an unfinished book. It ends—but it is not completed. Why? Certainly Luke could have gone back to the book in later years and written a postscript, even if the book was completed before A.D. 62. Why didn't he?

Because the Holy Spirit *deliberately intended* it to be unfinished!

The book of Acts is still being written. Like the Gospel of Luke, the book of Acts is yet another record of the things Jesus began both to do and to teach. Jesus isn't finished yet. He began His ministry in His human body, as recorded in the Gospels. He continued in His body, the church, through the book of Acts. And He continues His ministry today through you and me and every other believer on the planet.

> Jesus isn't finished yet. . . . He continues His ministry today through you and me and every other believer on the planet.

The book of Acts will be completed someday. And when it is completed, you and I will have a chance to read it in glory, in eternity, when the plan of God has been fulfilled.

What will your part be in that great story?

NOTES

NOTES

NOTES

NOTES

NOTES

NOTES

NOTES

NOTE TO THE READER

The publisher invites you to share your response to the message of this book by writing Discovery House Publishers, P.O. Box 3566, Grand Rapids, MI 49501, U.S.A. For information about other Discovery House books, music, videos, or DVDs, contact us at the same address or call 1-800-653-8333. Find us on the Internet at **http://www.dhp.org/** *or send e-mail to* **books@dhp.org***.*